Foreword

Any visitors to the tract of underused industrial land known as Mayfield could have been forgiven, until recently, for thinking that the area was of little historic interest, apart from the former Mayfield railway station and a largely culverted section of the River Medlock. This part of the city centre, however, has an incredibly rich history and its development from fields to factories in the late 18th century is a microcosm of industrial Manchester. Central to this was the Mayfield Printworks, which formed one of an important group of textile-finishing works that lined this section of the River Medlock, together with workers' housing and one of the earliest public baths and wash-houses to be built in Manchester. Much of the Mayfield Printworks was demolished in 1910 to make way for Mayfield railway station, which opened in 1910 as a relief station for Piccadilly but closed in 1960. The public baths were badly damaged during an aerial bombing raid in the Second World War, and the area suffered decline for the remainder of the 20th century, drifting gradually from public consciousness. This has now been reversed by a major regeneration scheme that is being brought forward by The Mayfield Partnership. The initial phase of this development has delivered the first new public park in Manchester city centre for more than a century. It is also wonderful to see a section of the River Medlock that has been hidden for most of the 20th century uncovered and once again made accessible for public benefit and enjoyment.

Development was preceded by archaeological excavations in 2020-21, which have unearthed the remarkable story of a 'hidden' corner of Manchester, charting its progress from semi-rural meadows to a thriving industrial quarter. The historic importance of Thomas Hoyle's textile printworks has been acknowledged for some time, but the excavations have facilitated a better understanding of its layout and has placed it in the context of its environs. Salford Archaeology is to be congratulated for compiling this well-illustrated, comprehensive and compelling account of the industrial origins and development of Mayfield.

Ian Miller
Lead Archaeologist
Greater Manchester Archaeological Advisory Service

Contents

Introduction

Prior to the 18th century, the area around Mayfield had retained a rural character. This changed in the latter half of the century, when two dyeworks were established on opposing banks of the River Medlock at Mayfield and Chapel Field. The success of these companies kickstarted the transformation of the area from open meadows to a bustling hive of industry.

Thomas Hoyle's printworks at Mayfield became one of Manchester's most famous textile-finishing works and throughout the 19th century was visited by industrialists and foreign dignitaries alike. On the opposite bank of the river in Ardwick stood another premier dyeworks, which also received accolades for its products. As these companies grew in size so too did their workforce, pulling in workers from across the country. Soon the river meadows and surrounding fields were masked by terraces of workers' housing, overshadowed by factory chimneys billowing smoke. The rise in population within and around the site – particularly low-quality workers' housing – led to the demand for public washing and bathing facilities. Some of the earliest in Manchester were established within the site. The opening of Mayfield baths in 1857, a vital amenity for the workers living close to the dyeworks and factories, made 'Mayfield' one of the city's first true industrial suburbs.

In spite of the long-term success of many of the enterprises within the site, as the domestic textile industry fell into decline, many of the city's other subsidiary industries suffered. By the turn of the 20th century, all of the former dyeworks buildings and many adjoining premises had been subsumed into one large factory producing rubber goods.

A small community of workers clung on, their houses visible on maps and aerial photographs from the early 20th century. These sub-standard houses were eventually swept away during slum clearances in the 1930s.

Moseley's India Rubber Works was a major employer from the mid-19th through to the late 20th century, producing a wide array of rubber goods. During its lifespan it provided work for thousands of individuals living in Ardwick and the surrounding area. Its eventual closure marked the end of manufacturing within the site and the beginning of its decline. As a result of its economic downturn, this part of the city has frequently been overlooked in regard to its contribution to the urban landscape and more generally in terms of its industrial history. This has also perhaps been exasperated by its current peripheral nature in relation to the commercial hub of the modern city. With work now fully underway to regenerate the area, its position is on the up.

In the winter of 2020-21, a series of large-scale excavations were undertaken ahead of the site's regeneration. The investigation was funded by The Mayfield Partnership – comprised of U+I, Manchester City Council, Transport for Greater Manchester and LCR Groundworks for the extensive Mayfield Park – Manchester's first public park in over a century – provided an opportunity to examine parts of the former dyeworks, tannery, houses and public baths.

Four open-area excavations totalling 3925m^2 were completed by Salford Archaeology. Throughout the project guidance was received from the Greater Manchester Archaeological Advisory Service (Norman Redhead and Ian Miller) with assistance provided by P.P. O'Connor, who oversaw the bulk earthworks and civil engineering onsite.

Left: Street parade promoting Moseley Tyres and Mackintoshes Right: View across Moseley's India Rubber Works, looking toward London Road Station (©Manchester Image Libraries)

Early Settlement

Occupying land on both the northern and southern banks of the River Medlock, the site straddles the historic boundary between the townships of Manchester and Ardwick. Originally, Ardwick was one of eight hamlets forming the manor of Manchester. The placename has Old English origins; it was first mentioned in 1282 as *Atheriswyke*, which is thought to derive from an abbreviation of the name Aethelred, perhaps after the king, and *wic* meaning a farm or hamlet.

The population of Ardwick during the late medieval period was relatively small, containing just ten households in the 14th century. In 1320-2 one inhabitant, Richard Akke a villein, held land in exchange for services to the lord of Manchester. From the middle of the 14th century land and property within the hamlet of Ardwick began to be leased rather than held *in lieu* of services and rental payments made in monetary form.

A perspective of the houses at Ardwick Green, 1762
(All images in chapter © Manchester Libraries, Information and Archives)

In 1357, the baron of Manchester granted the hamlet of Ardwick together with Bradford and other lands to Thomas de Booth of Barton, who had previously leased the land.
The Booth family retained the estate until the end of the 16th century, at which time the ancestral lands inherited by Dorothy Booth passed through marriage to John Molyneux. The Booth estate in turn passed to their only child Bridget Molyneux, who married Thomas Charnock. In 1636, Thomas Charnock sold the 'manors of Over and Lower Ardwick' to Samuel Birch.

The hearth tax of 1666 indicates there were 34 hearths liable to duties, seven of which were within the principal residence of the township, a hall owned by Samuel Birch. Of the remaining 24 hearths, it is possible to infer that the population had risen slightly from the 14th century. Indeed, by the Tudor period the numbers living in the hamlet had grown as such to cause nuisances within the settlement; contemporary accounts refer to 'wild women, disorderly houses, children playing giddy gaddy and too many dunghills in the road'.

The economy within Ardwick had developed and surviving probate records from the 16th and 17th centuries furnish evidence of an emerging textile industry. One of the earliest records of this period is the will and testament of Edward Richardson, a wealthy chapman who died in 1591. His personal estate was valued at £161 12 s 1d and included 'loomes and reades and their furnyture', quantities of bleached and unbleached linen yarn and sackcloth – a coarse fabric similar to hessian. Intriguingly, Edward Richardson was known by the alias Edward Wolworkes and was evidently engaged in the production and trade of linen. The persistence of this cottage industry in Ardwick is attested by the occurrence of websters and weavers throughout the following century.

Saturday afternoon at Ardwick Green

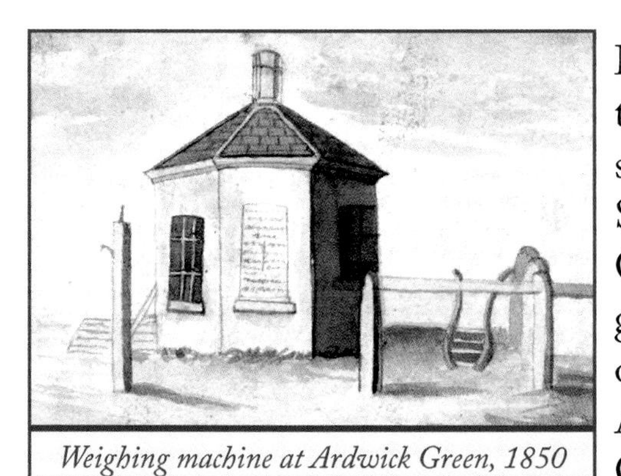

Weighing machine at Ardwick Green, 1850

Moving forward to the 18th century, a notable settlement that had coalesced around St Thomas' chapel in the southern part of the township, which had been built by Samuel Birch in 1740. The church lay adjacent to Ardwick Green, a private garden, which served its residents. The green was first laid out in the late 18th century as an ornamental park, with a man-made pond at its centre. Although little more than a village, the status of Ardwick Green was elevated and considered by contemporaries to be genteel. It was referred to by Engels in the 1830s as having 'free, wholesome country air' and 'fine comfortable homes', and continued to attract merchants and other prosperous members of society well into the mid-19th century.

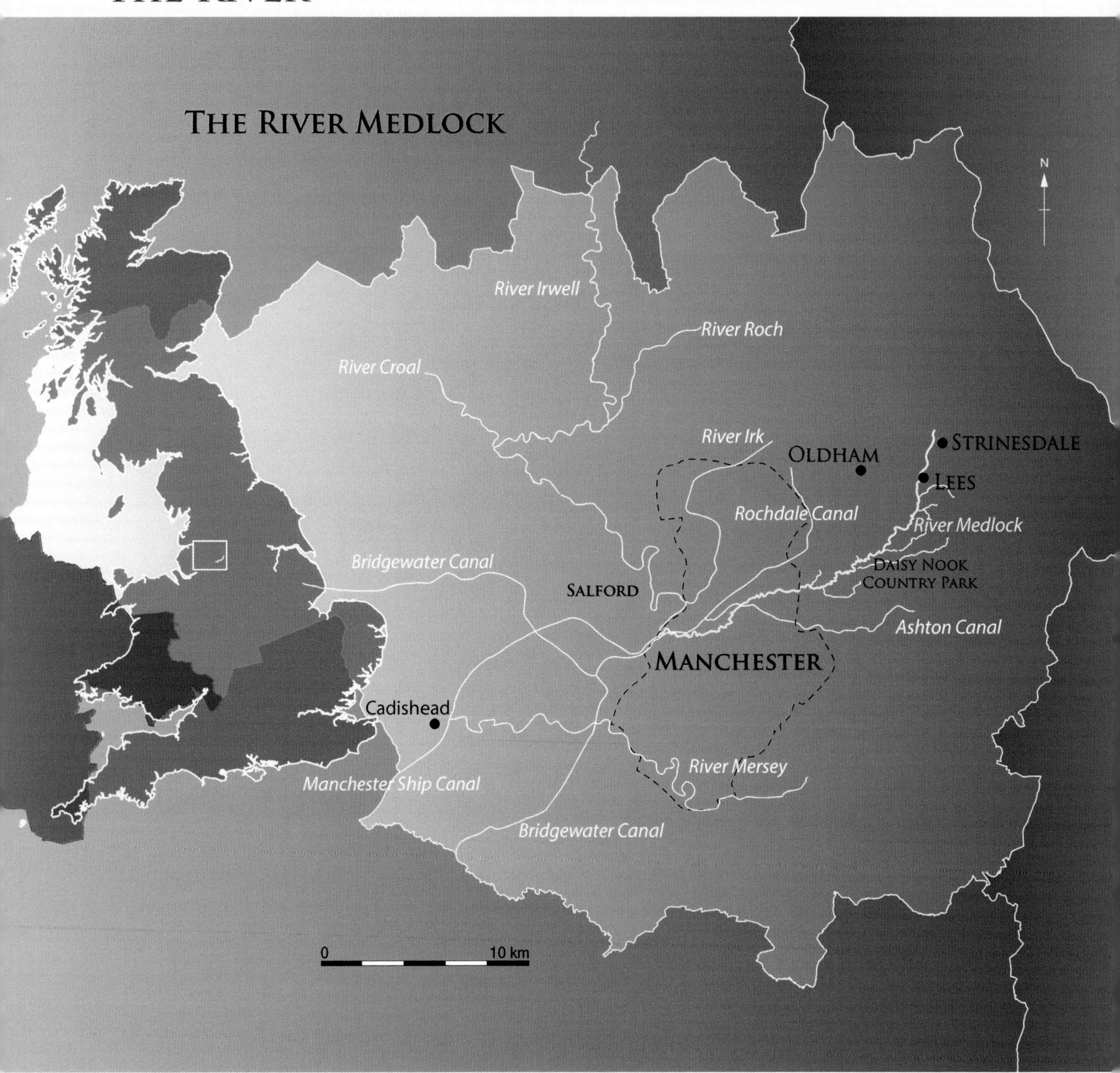

Map showing the course of the River Medlock, from its source, rising in the hills that surround Strinesdale, to where it meets the River Irwe

Emanating in the foothills of the Pennines at Strinedale, near Oldham, the River Medlock winds its way through the eastern and southern suburbs of Manchester until its confluence with the Irwell. Much of the upper reaches of the river have maintained a semi-natural state, characterised by steeply incised and wooded banks. Upon approaching the more urbanised heart of the city, it becomes decidedly clear that the river has been intensely modified. Hemmed in by centuries of building, large stretches of the river are culverted, canalised and largely hidden from view. This was no better illustrated than at Mayfield. It had once provided a backbone to the site's development but was built over by bridges, flanked by river walls and overshadowed by buildings. Until recently, only glimpses of the river could be had from vantage points at various crossings.

The River Medlock – the river that flows through the meadows – takes its name from the Old English for meadow: *medlacu*. The name conjures up a picture of the bucolic landscape that existed around Manchester prior to the Industrial Revolution.

The antiquarian John Whitaker envisaged the countryside in antiquity with its '[rivers] Irwell, Medlock, and Irk indented by knolls, doughs, and little gullies of picturesque red rock…overhung with spreading trees, and their crests marked with broom, heather, and gorse'. The rivers were prone to bursting their banks, and the rough ground on the floodplains and surrounding moors were host to wild boar and cattle.

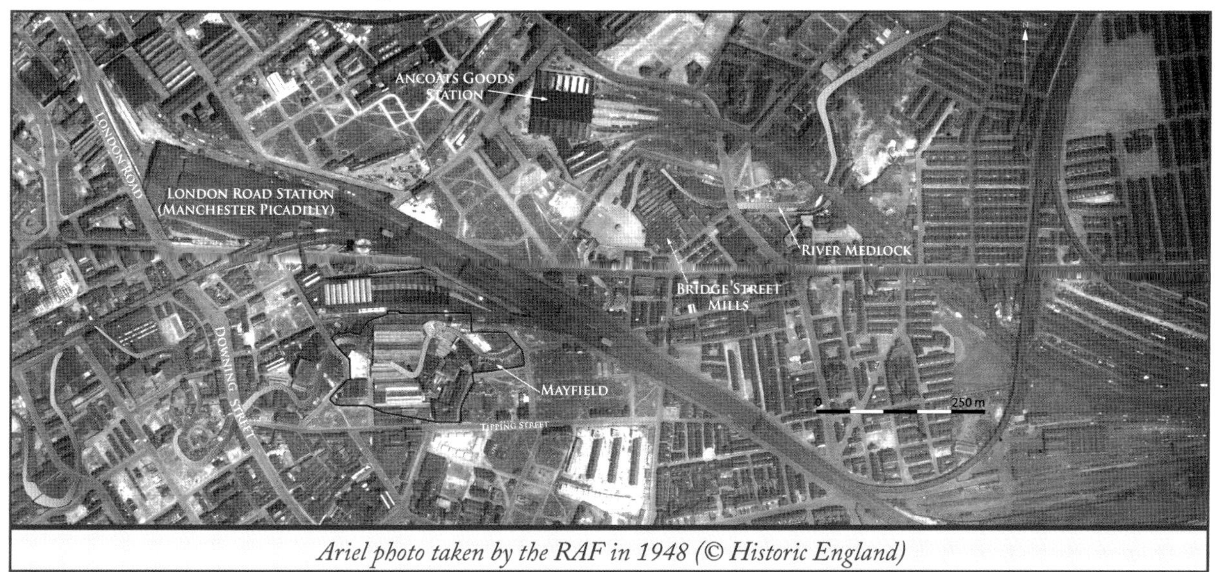

Ariel photo taken by the RAF in 1948 (© Historic England)

Fishing for lampreys in a river
(Source: Tacuinum Sanitatis)

Before the widespread construction of bridges in the 17th and 18th centuries, the river was primarily crossed by a series of fords. One such ford has been inferred from a 13th-century fieldname *Twantirford* meaning 'the crooked ford', located somewhere in the vicinity of Ardwick. It may be that the location of this ford coincided with the projected alignment of the Roman road from Buxton to Manchester, which is thought to pass by Ardwick Bridge – a point where the road curiously changes direction, perhaps giving rise to the 'crooked' element of the name.

One of the earliest references to the river concerns its exploitation as a fishery in the 14th century; at this time, the baron of Manchester presided over the fishing rights in the Medlock, Irk and Gorebrook, which collectively were worth a shilling *per annum*. The apparent prevalence of fish in the river attest to its cleanliness and health before it was overwhelmed by pollution in the 19th century.

Viaduct over the River Medlock and Ashton Canal, on the Ardwick Branch Railway
(printed Maclure, Macdonald and Macgregor, Liverpool, London and Glasgow circa 1846)

One of the earliest industries to develop in the catchment of the Medlock Valley was the quarrying and burning of limestone to make quicklime for building. The discovery of old workings and tools at the Ardwick Lime Works in the 19th century were interpreted as Roman in date. Cross-analysis of mortar from the Roman fort at Castlefield and samples from the seams in Ardwick confirmed similarities in their composition. Whilst the Roman origins of this industry seem plausible, the first historical reference to lime burning dates to 1322, when a 'kiln at the Ancoates' reached by means of a 'stany gate [stoney road]' existed. Other lime kilns were subsequently founded downstream at Knot Mill in the 17th century and alongside the Bridgewater Canal in the 18th century.

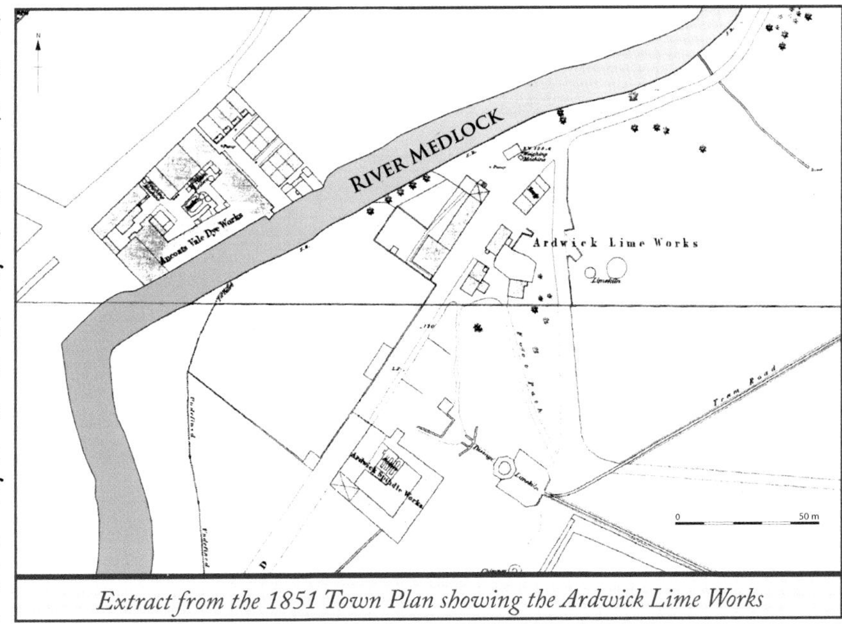

Extract from the 1851 Town Plan showing the Ardwick Lime Works

In the late 18th century, the River Medlock resumed importance, becoming an artery for the first wave of textile mills and finishing works. William Yates' county map of 1786 provides some indication of where these formative sites were located. Manchester's earliest textile mill, Garrett Mill, founded in c.1760 on a prominent meander of the river can be seen on Yates' map.

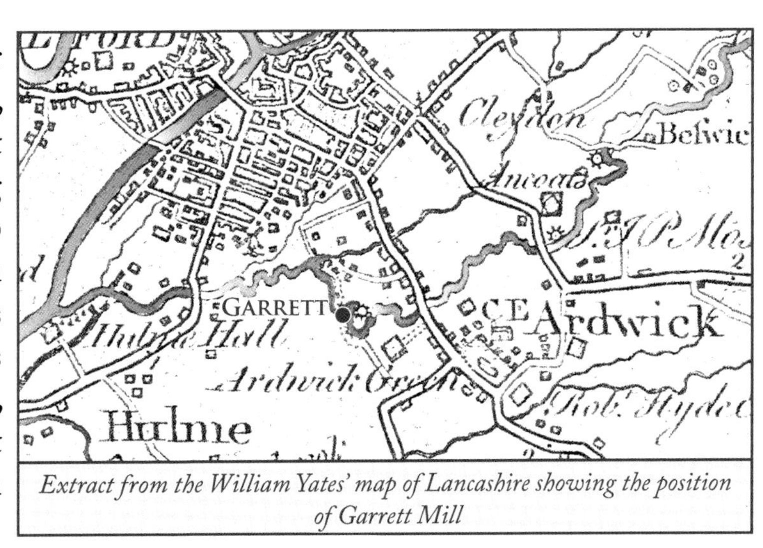

Extract from the William Yates' map of Lancashire showing the position of Garrett Mill

The premises were first established as a silk mill by Mr Gartside, who had intended to run the mill machinery from a waterwheel, although his initial efforts proved unsuccessful. By the early 1780s, the premises had been converted to cotton-spinning and were owned by 'Messrs Thackeray & Whitehead'. Attempts were again made to harness power from the river, to run the mill machinery based on Sir Richard Arkwright's water frame pioneered at Cromford Mill in Derbyshire; Garrett Mill may even have been up and running before Arkwright's own mill at Shudehill in Manchester, which opened in 1782-3.

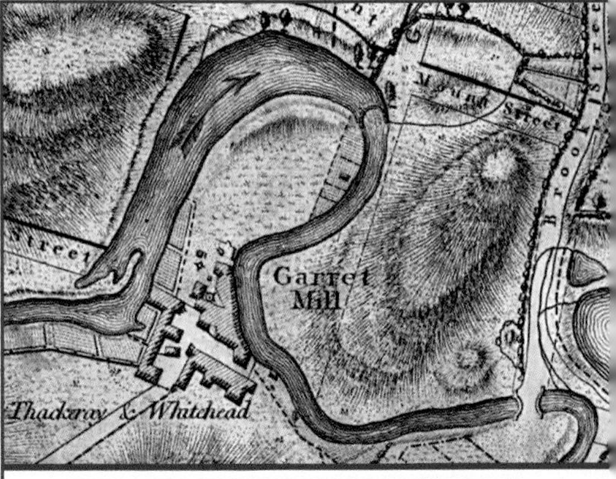

Extract from Laurent's map of 1793 showing Garrett Mill

Concentrations of subsidiary factory based activity along the riverbanks were captured on William Green's map from 1794. In particular, the stretch of river between Ardwick Bridge (now London Road) and Ancoats Bridge (Great Ancoats Street) boasted no less than five dyeworks, constituting a hub for this important branch of the textile industry. The density of dyeworks in this area would have sustained a sizeable enclave of dyers. The proximity of the firms undoubtedly fostered competition, perhaps contributing to the elevated status and renown of the works in the following centuries.

From historic mapping and the contemporary documentary resource, it is clear the course of the river adjacent to Hoyle's print and dyeworks at Mayfield was altered during this period. A vertical line crossing the river marks the position of a weir, which would have directed water into an artificial channel to power a waterwheel. The weir and waterwheel are both denoted on Laurent's map of 1793 and were probably relied upon until the sale of the waterwheel pit wheel, which were advertised not long after in the *Manchester Mercury* on 3rd November 1795.

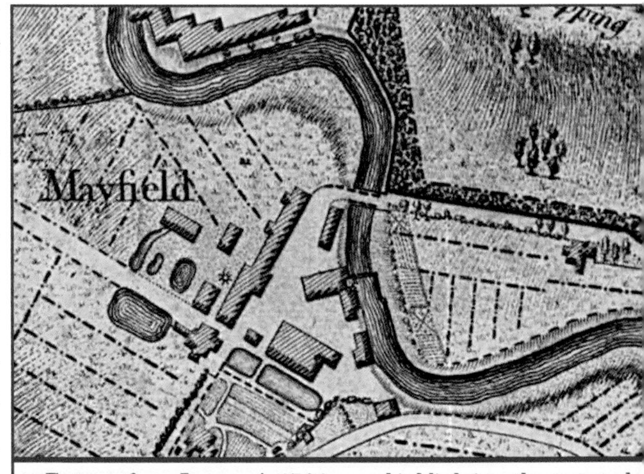

Extract from Laurent's 1793 map highlighting the waterwhe and weir associated with the Mayfield works

As might be expected, heightened industrial activity along the river brought with it pollution. This was by no means instantaneous, and the cleanliness of the river lasted longer than might be expected. This stretch of the river was remembered by Alfred Neild (of the Mayfield Printworks), who was born in 1822, as a 'large extent of fields, running along the banks of the River Medlock, which was then sufficiently attractive for boys to bathe in'. Another contemporary writer recalled the days when the river ran as a 'fine clear stream at Ardwick Bridge' where he had 'used to water the horse in' but had soon been relegated to the 'filthy Medlock'. As more and more industrial waste was discharged into the river, it became not just dirty but toxic. In 1884, a boy named John Tarpey got into difficulty whilst bathing in the river and accidentally swallowed some water, which in turn led to a swift death from poisoning.

Pollution was not the only way man-made developments had affected the river. After sections of the river had been culverted in the 1820s, flooding risks were increased and, in the summer of 1857, the river burst its banks with disastrous effects; this forced the culvert to be rebuilt and land on either side raised. Two decades later came the flood of 1872, which wrought destruction of various properties alongside the river, and was even immortalised in a ballad 'The Great Flood'. One of the properties that was damaged was Thomas Hoyle & Son's printworks, where the river 'overthrew a high wall' putting a temporary stop to work.

Above: River Medlock flowing underneath Bridgewater Viaduct.
Right: Castlefield Basin, where the River Medlock meets the Bridgewater Canal, 2020

Dyeworks and Printworks

A number of dyeworks and printworks were established on the banks of the River Medlock during the 18th century. These took full advantage of the ready availability of water and open land, both much needed for dyeing and bleaching cloth. Historic maps reveal some of the names of those engaged in this industry: Thomas Hoyle; Edge & Beswick; and John and James Entwistle.

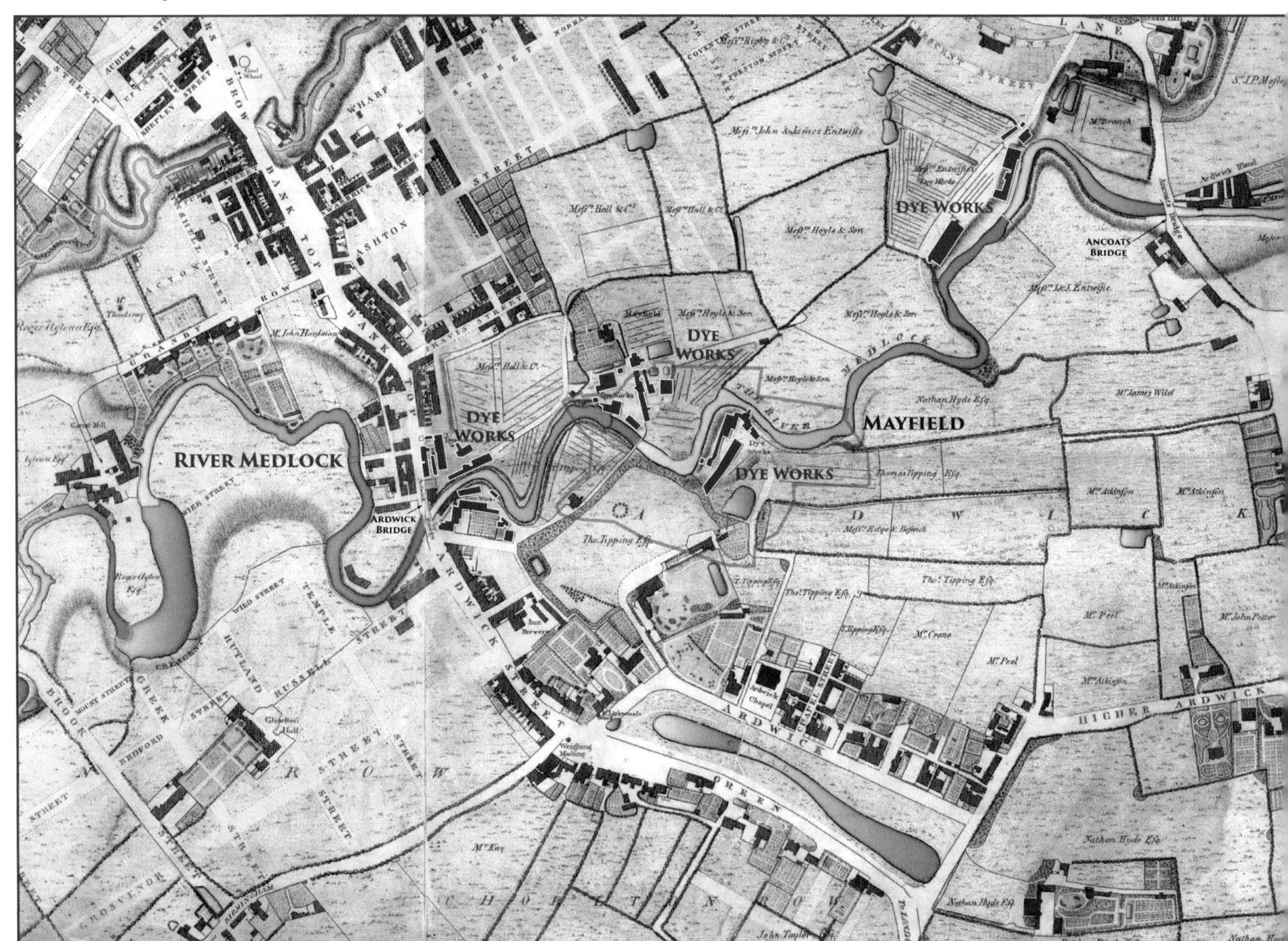

Concentration of dyeworks between Ardwick and Ancoats bridges, and the Mayfield site location superimposed on William Green's Plan of Manchester and Salford, 1787–94

Traditional methods of dyeing involved steeping cloth in a mixture of colouring agent and water in a vat known as a dye bath. In factory settings, a belt-driven roller was commonly installed above the dye bath, to allow the cloth to be dipped in and out of the liquid.

From the late 18th century – when the first dyeworks were established on the Medlock – until the mid-19th century, the dyes used to colour yarn and cloth were sourced primarily from natural substances, be it animal, vegetable or mineral. The surviving dye recipes and relevant newspaper accounts reveal that madder, indigo, fustic and shumac were among the vegetable dyes commonly used, together with cochineal, a colourant derived from a South American beetle. Other ingredients of the time included Brazil wood and logwood. The process of converting the natural colouring matter into dyes was complex and required inordinate quantities of material to be processed and concentrated down. The trade in some of these exotic dyestuffs, particularly indigo from the Americas, signals a dark side to the dyeing industry, as it benefitted heavily from the slave trade between Europe, Africa and the Americas.

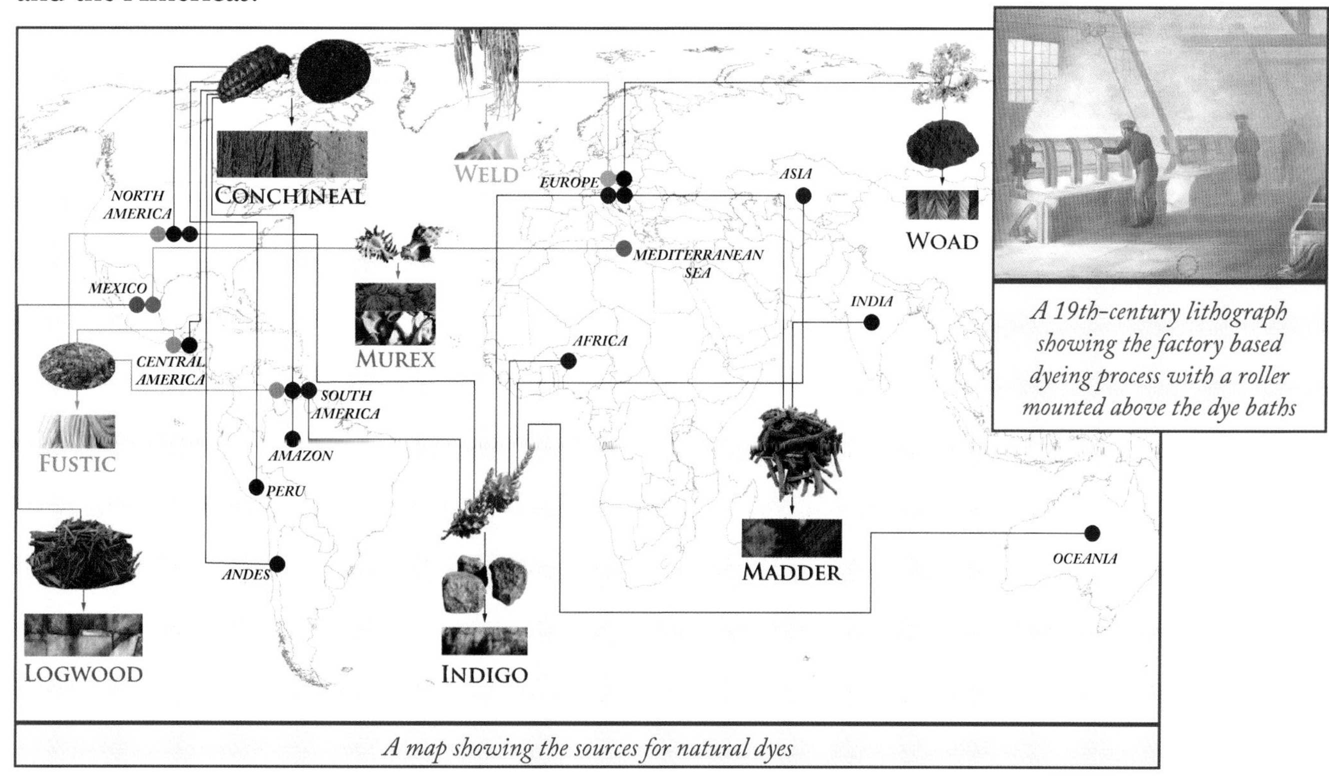

A 19th-century lithograph showing the factory based dyeing process with a roller mounted above the dye baths

A map showing the sources for natural dyes

Often natural dyes did not adhere to the cloth easily, requiring the addition of other substances known as mordants, which fixed the dyes to the fabric. Alum, iron liquor and copperas appear in the dye recipes of John Graham, Mayfield's chemist. Whilst alum was sourced from further afield, copperas (iron sulphate) also known as green vitriol could be produced locally. A copperas works in Droylsden, around 4.8km from the site was investigated in 2021. It was originally founded around 1800. At the site, mineral pyrites were transformed through weathering in ponds and heating in ovens to produce a black substance, which was used a variety of recipes, including alongside indigo to make 'china blue' dye.

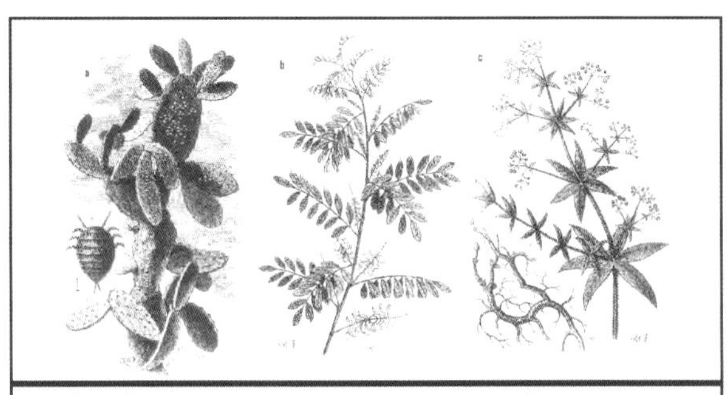

From left to right: cochineal, indigo plant and madderroot

In light of the expense attached to exotic dyes, sourced from far flung reaches of the globe, attempts were made to find alternative man-made substances. One of the earliest synthetic dyes – aniline – was discovered by chance in 1856. The trade in natural dyestuffs was eventually eclipsed by the domestic production of chemical dyes, which lowered costs and offered a wide palette of colours. Synthetic dyes often relied on the use of hazardous chemicals such as aniline and cyanide, which were detrimental to the health of the workers who handled them, as well as polluting the rivers into which they were frequently discharged.

Base of a conical oven at the Droylsden copperas works

One of the earliest dyeworks in this area, founded around 1780, was situated on the southern bank of the River Medlock and belonged to 'Messrs Edge & Beswick'. Maps produced in 1793 and 1794 capture the site at an early stage of its development. After only a decade, the dyeworks consisted of a haphazard cluster of riverside buildings with a portion of the northern range extending partway across the river; whilst this may signify that the owners harnessed the water's power to run machinery within the works, it remains a strong possibility the building over the river channel was intended for 'conditioning' the cloth by storing it in a damp environment.

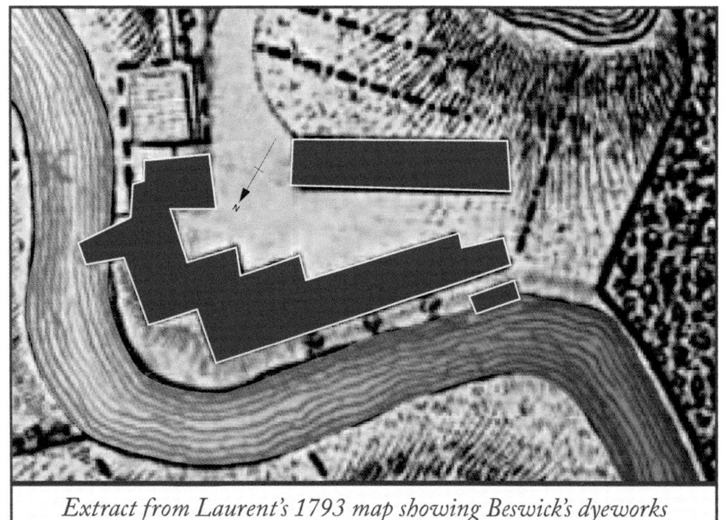

Extract from Laurent's 1793 map showing Beswick's dyeworks

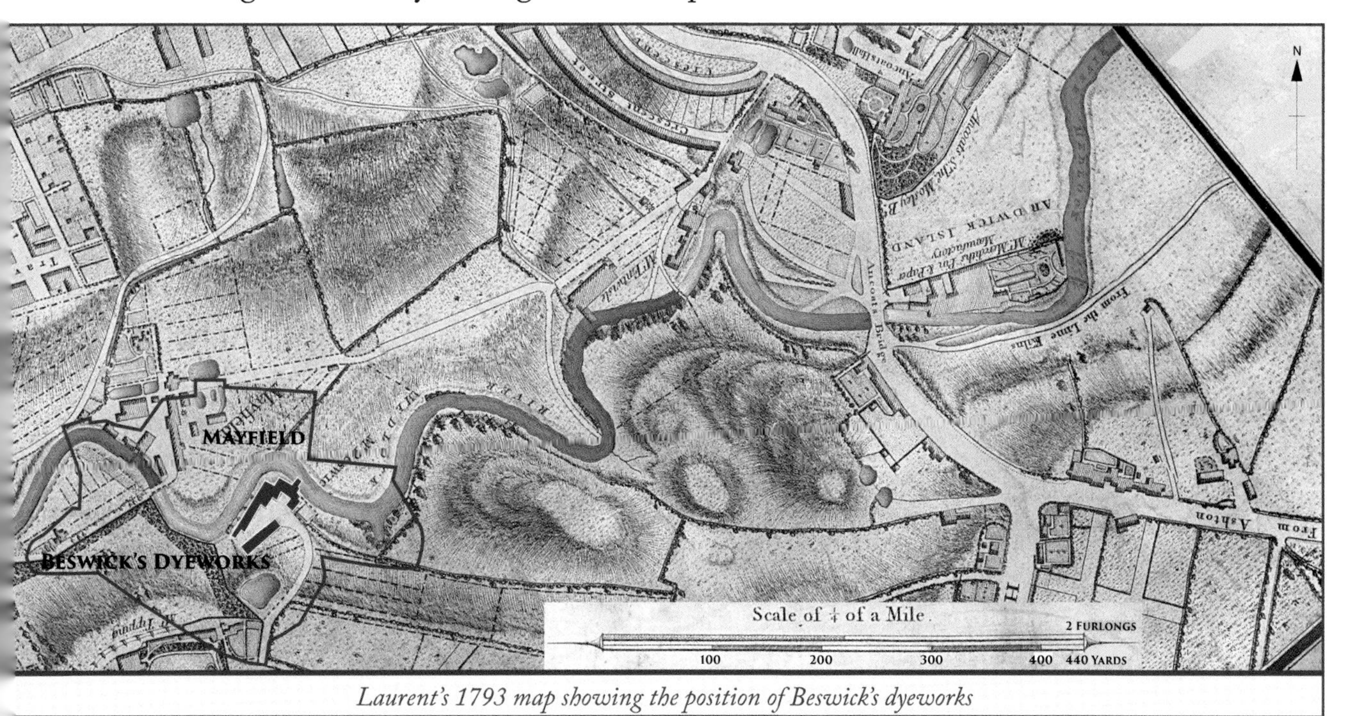

Laurent's 1793 map showing the position of Beswick's dyeworks

The partners responsible for the dyework's inception were Ardwick-based dyers Thomas and John Beswick in partnership with the Edge family of Manchester. Richard and Thomas Edge were first and foremost fustian manufacturers and were members of the Manchester Committee of Trade in the 1780s. At a time of supposed friction and tension between different branches of the textile industry, the commercial partnership between the well-established manufacturers-come-wholesalers, and emerging artisans, provides a clear example of cooperation.

Prior to this, Richard and Thomas Edge had been in partnership with their brothers James and John, yarn merchants with premises on St James Square, Manchester. They all followed in the footsteps of their father, William Edge, a fustian maker who was active in Manchester from as early as 1744 and was responsible for establishing one of the town's earliest cotton mills, in 1783. Edge's mill was situated on the River Irk close to its confluence with the River Irwell, and comprised a three-storey factory that was added to an existing corn mill.

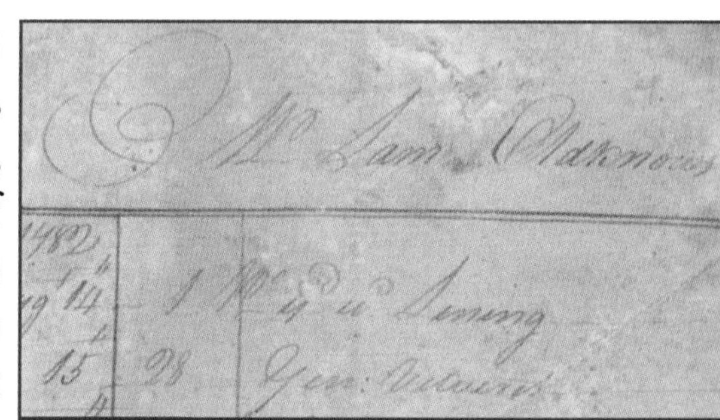

Fragment of an account book described as 'Mr Saml Oldknow's [Account] with Edge & Beswick' GB 133 SO/10/1 (© John Ryland's Library, University of Manchester)

'Messrs Edge & Beswick' of Ardwick were operational from c. 1781 to 1797, styling themselves first as 'fustian dressers and dyers' and latterly as 'kerseymere printers', the latter being a finer grade of cloth. Though little evidence survives to embellish their activities with any detail, a fragment of an account book dating from 1782-3 indicates they bleached and dyed cloth for Samuel Oldknow – a renowned manufacturer of quality cotton calico and muslin in Stockport and Mellor. This rare piece of evidence serves to demonstrate their growing clientele and overall success of the enterprise. This business continued under the name 'Edge & Beswick' until c. 1797 but appears to have later been disbanded, a choice perhaps compounded by the death of Thomas Beswick in 1795.

A new partnership 'Beswick & Holt' was established in the years following Thomas' death. This venture, seemingly under the direction of John Beswick and Joseph Holt was however short-lived, lasting only until 1810.

In 1809, the company held celebrations for George III's 49th Jubilee and 'feasted their workers in a truly hospitable and liberal manner'. By the following year, however, the partners announced they were closing their business, a decision possibly driven by John Beswick's declining health. Auctions first advertised the sale of all the company's dyeing equipment and later its land and property. This included a house occupied by Joseph Holt and 'those very extensive dye houses, works and buildings at Ardwick aforesaid, lately in occupation of Messrs Beswicks and Holt...in complete repair, and advantageously situated for carrying on the dyeing business on the most extensive scale' (*Manchester Mercury*, 17 July 1810). John Beswick lived on for a few years, until 1812; his obituary appearing in the *Manchester Mercury* read: '[died] after a lingering illness, Mr John Beswick of Ardwick, dyer; much respected'.

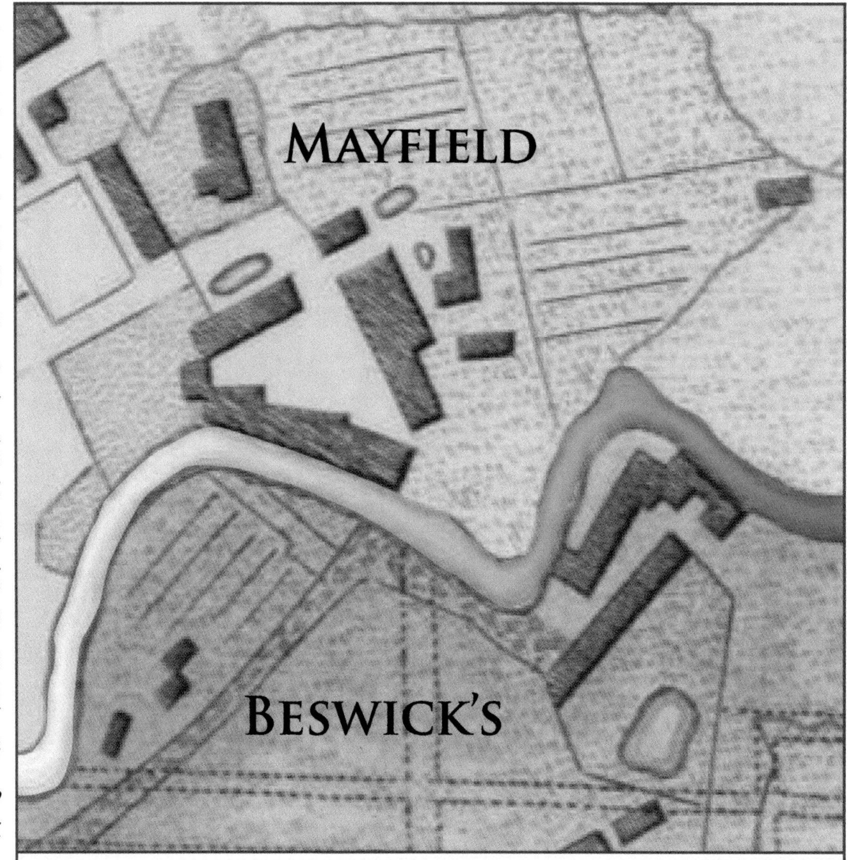

Extract from Dean and Pigot's map of Manchester showing the Beswick's dyeworks in 1809 around the time the partnership of Beswick & Holt was forged (© University of Manchester)

Between 1810 and 1812 the dyeworks were sold and divided into two plots. As a result of this division, the southern part of the complex continued as a dyeworks, henceforth known as Ardwick Dyeworks, whilst the northern group of buildings known collectively as the Chapelfield Works was occupied by a range of businesses and factories, only resuming a role as a dyeworks for a brief period of time.

The Longsdons

The Ardwick Dyeworks was owned and occupied for two decades by Peter Longsdon (1770-1848), his half-nephew James Longsdon (1794-1874) and Peter's son Frederick Longsdon (1809-).

Peter was the youngest of eight sons of Thomas Longsdon (1706-80) of Little Longstone, Derbyshire, whose family-held estate had existed from the 12th century. After the decades-long decline of the family's wealth, Thomas' sons began rebuilding their fortune first through pastoral farming by capitalising on the increase in the value of wool in the early 19th century and later through investment in the region's burgeoning textile industry. Thomas' eldest son by his first marriage, James Longsdon (1745-1821), was at the vanguard of this shift from farming to textiles, forming a partnership with the cotton merchant Andrew Morewood with whom he opened-up a trading agency in St Petersburg, Russia. He later made the move to manufacturing, building a carding mill, warehouse and bleaching croft in Great Longstone in the High Peak.

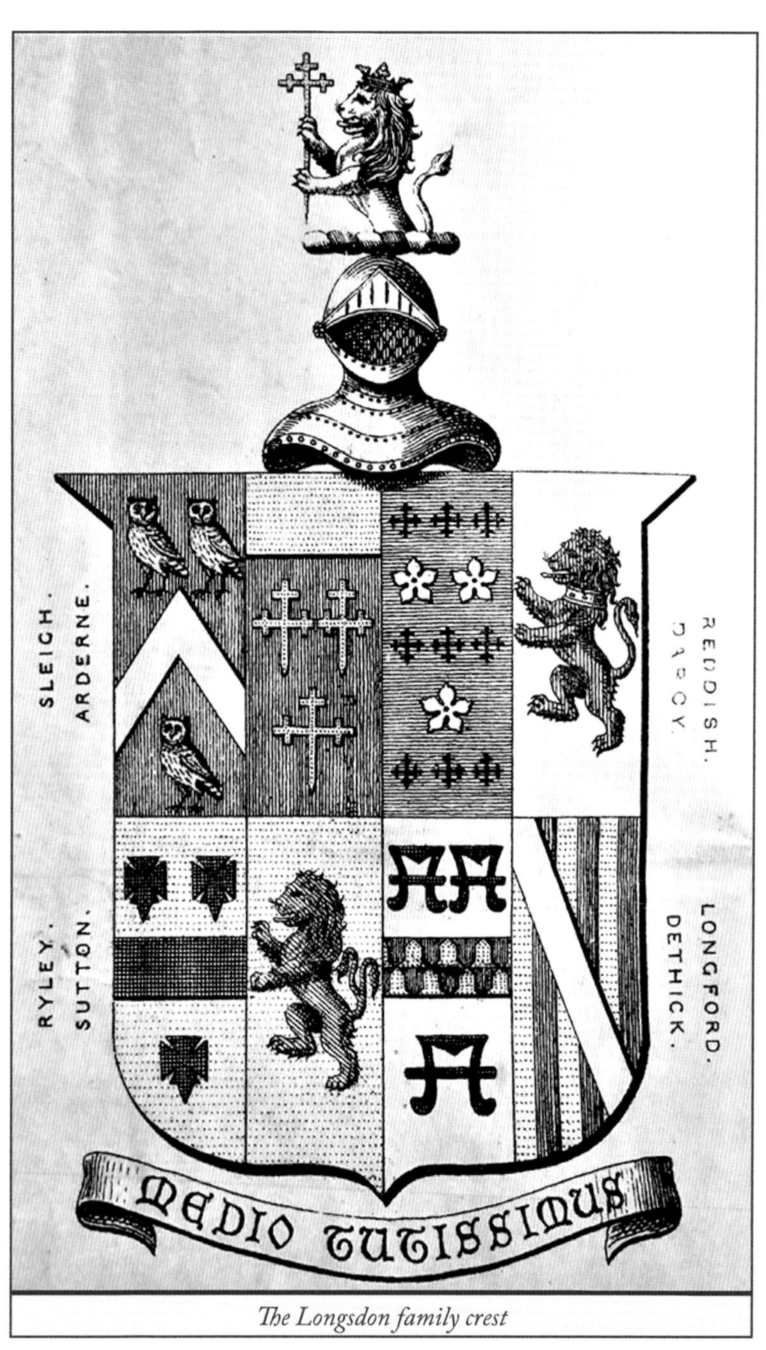

The Longsdon family crest

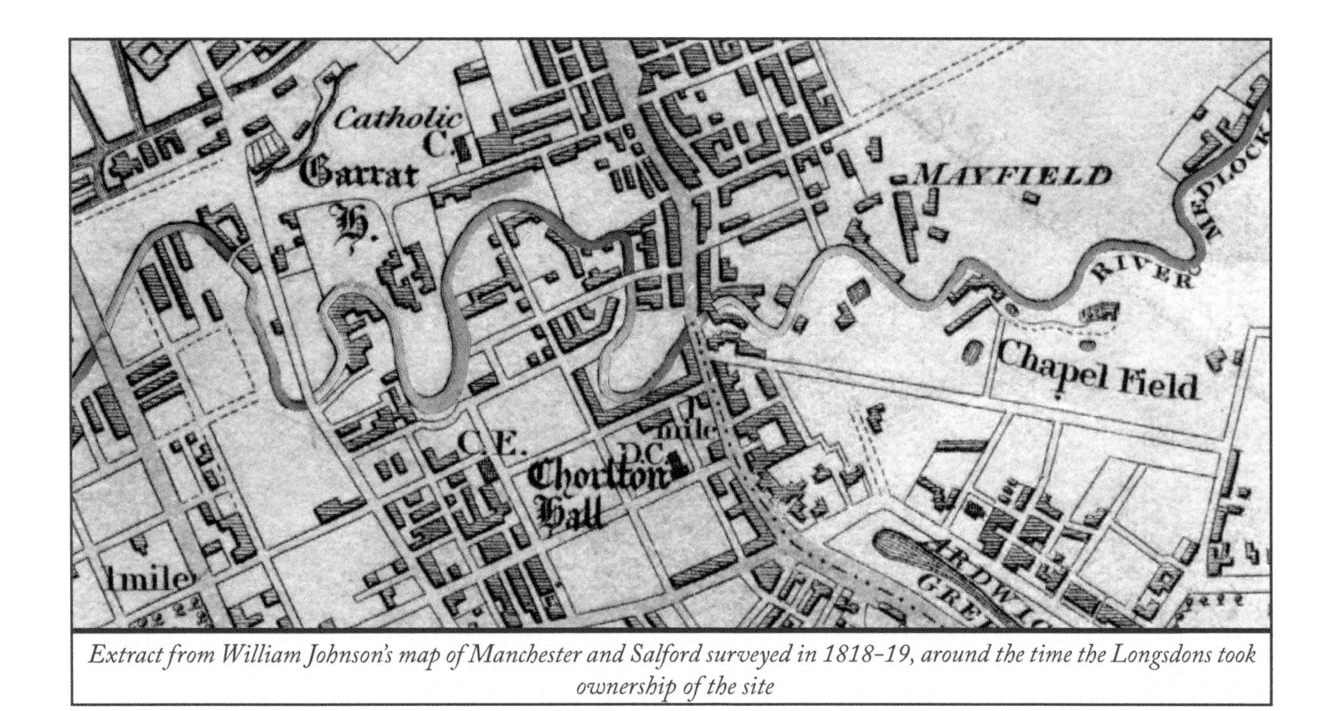

Extract from William Johnson's map of Manchester and Salford surveyed in 1818-19, around the time the Longsdons took ownership of the site

Thomas Longsdon's half-brothers, Matthew and Peter, followed suit, entering into business as cotton merchants with G. Willion in Manchester and London. James Longsdon withdrew from textile manufacturing in 1812 following bankruptcy; Peter and his brother Matthew however continued trading.

Peter Longsdon and his half-nephew James were the ones who made the move to dyeing and finishing fabric. Peter was first registered as a dyer in Ardwick in 1818, although he may have taken up shop sometime after 1812. According to rate books in 1821, James Longsdon was the owner and Peter Longsdon, the occupier; the dyeworks were then assessed at £100. From 1822, Peter took on sole ownership of the premises, which were run jointly by the partners for a further seven years before Peter took eventual control in the 1830s, whilst James returned to Derbyshire, working as a road surveyor.

NOTICE is hereby given, that the Partnership heretofore subsisting between us the undersigned, and carried on at Ardwick and at Manchester, in the County of Lancaster, was dissolved by mutual consent on the 30th day of June last: As witness our hands this 31st day of July 1829.

Peter Longsdon.
James Longsdon.

Excerpt from the London Gazette (1829) notifying the dissolution of Peter and James Longsdon's partnership

A fleeting partnership between Longdson and John M. Clegg lasted from 1834-6. Peter resumed sole propriety and took on his son Frederick, trading under the name 'P. Longsdon & Son'. Peter and Frederick were responsible for erecting a public baths on Tipping Street in 1837 – a precursor to the longer-lived and more famous Mayfield baths.

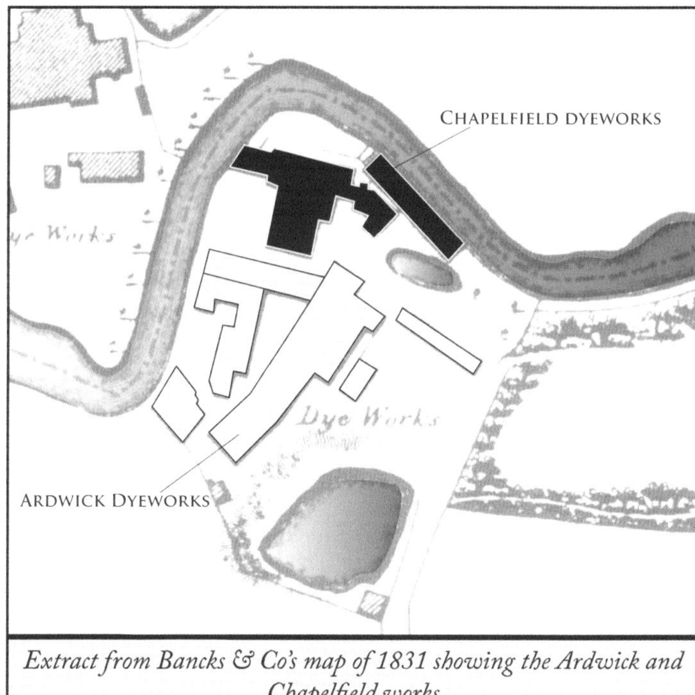

Extract from Bancks & Co's map of 1831 showing the Ardwick and Chapelfield works

Towards the end of their time as dyers in Ardwick, a partnership was formed between Frederick Longsdon and John Booth and three other partners, trading as 'Longsdon Booth & Co' In 1837, following the bankruptcy of the firm, the dyeworks and other property were conveyed by the owners to pay off creditors. The land and buildings were later sold by private auction in 1838: the premises consisted of 'extensive dyehouses, with good stone vats, dryhouses, excellent steam engine of 14 horses' power, boiler' together with a 'large reservoir, with a plentiful supply of water'.

Peter's son Frederick Longsdon took advantage of the experience he gained in the dyeing trade and on went on to become a 'drysalter' or trader of dyestuffs. He was evidently successful, moving his family and father to Old Trafford Hall. Peter died aged 79 in 1848 and was buried in Chorlton-cum-Hardy, an affluent leafy suburb of Manchester. In spite of his desire to be buried in Manchester an epitaph was added to his father Thomas' grave in Little Longston; it read: "To the memory of PETER youngest son of the above who died at Old Trafford near Manchester November 15th 1848 in his 79th year."

William Andrew and Richard Jones

Empty rate book entries for the Ardwick Dyeworks reveal the premises were left vacant for several years after the Longsdens departed. In 1844, the dyeworks was leased to 'W. Andrew & Co', who quickly became well-established in the trade. By the mid-19th century 'specimens of their dye and Mellowdew's patent cotton velvet' featured in the Great Exhibition (of the Works of Industry of All Nations) of 1851. In the same year, they dyed and finished a patented 'cotton velvet', which met with approval from Queen Victoria.

After nearly decade, in 1853, William Andrew & Co bought the premises from the assignees of Peter Longsdon. It was around this time the firm took on a new partner, Richard Jones. Both their names appear in the rate book entries from 1853 to 1870.

Several years later, in the summer of 1857, the Medlock burst its banks, wreaking havoc for businesses along the river. A report of the flood is particularly revealing when it comes to the contents of the dyeworks. The mention of 'drying cylinders' in the 'stove rooms' is a good indicator that the process of drying the finished cloth – previously undertaken outside – had been brought inside. It is also evident from the report that vegetable dyes such as shumac, fustic and indigo were still being used.

Richard Jones played an increased role in the firm as time went on, representing the company in both financial and philanthropic matters. It comes as no surprise that by 1871, Richard Jones and his son Charles had taken over the business at Tipping Street, then known as Richard Jones & Son; William Andrew, however, retained ownership of the premises.

In 1872, a fire broke out at the dyeworks. It was extinguished before it resulted in irreparable damage. Hundreds of pounds worth of calico was damaged or destroyed but was covered by the company's insurance. They recovered and continued trading until c.1876 when it was absorbed into the growing factory complex of D. Moseley's India Rubber Works.

The Chapelfield Works came into being in c.1812 following the division of the dyeworks. It was acquired by David Dockray, who leased the buildings to various concerns. Dockray was active in the textile industry as a woollen and cotton manufacturer and lived at Ardwick Green. Like Thomas Hoyle, he was a Quaker; in 1805, he married Abigail Benson, who later became a prominent minister in the church.

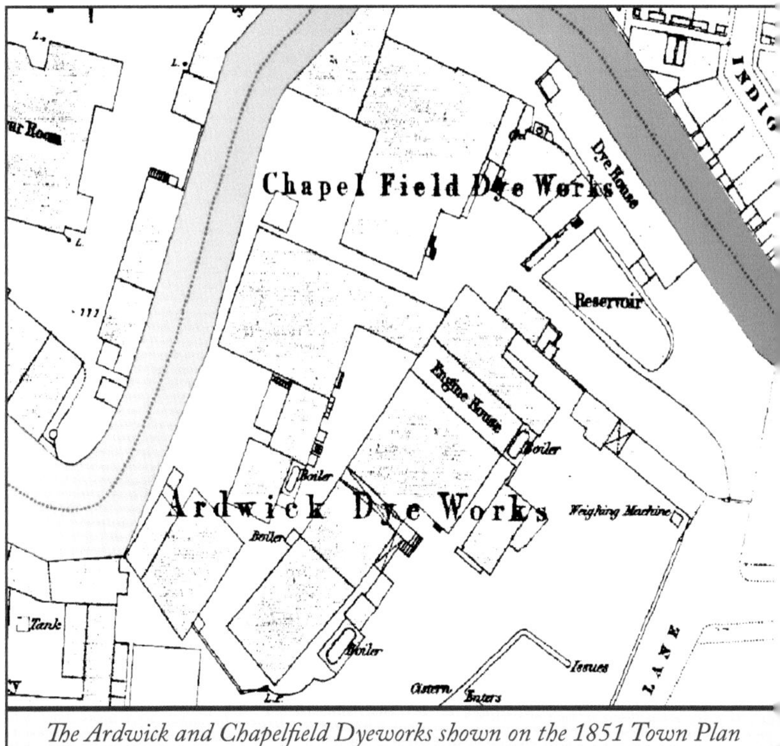

The Ardwick and Chapelfield Dyeworks shown on the 1851 Town Plan

Textile finishing and dyeing continued alongside metalworking and other industries at the works. According to Pigot's 1837 national directory Joseph Wells & Co, styling themselves as 'stiffeners', were occupants of the Chapelfield Works. Not long after this, an article in the *Manchester Courier and Lancashire General Advertiser* from the 9th February 1839, advertised the Chapelfield Works to be sold or let. Within the article, the former occupant was stated as being a William Wells, who used the Chapelfield Works 'for the general business of machine making'. The works was described as having 'engine power, a plentiful supply of water and good lights'. It stated that the works were 'fitted up with a 17-horse power steam engine, mill gearing, steam pipes, gas piping and lights'. During the late 1830s, the site occupied 3075 square yards of land, covering 132 yards of river frontage.

By 1846, the Chapelfield Works were occupied by another company, Hordern & Riding, who used the buildings for manufacturing cotton. After Riding's death the works was leased to Mr Thomas Barlow, who, as stated in the *Manchester Courier and Lancashire General Advertiser* on the 13th June 1846, had intentions to continue the business under the same name.

Around the same time that textile production was going on, so too was dyeing. An article published in 1849 listed the contents of the Chapelfield Works, recently occupied by the fustian dyer Mr Ebenezer Heap that were to be sold in auction. These included 'a quantity of dyeing utensils' such as welling pan, copper and iron rollers, lever squeezers, wooden cisterns and sundry dye tubs. Steam for the mechanical plant was raised in a waggon-shaped wrought-iron steam boiler, measuring 15ft. 6in by 5ft (4.72m x 1.52m).

From 1845, David Moseley – an India Rubber producer – began occupying part of the Chapelfield Works. The other tenants at this time ran a textile-finishing works, specialised in stretching and stiffening cloth. Wheelan's 1853 directory indicates other parts of the site were let to a whole host of other businesses, including a wiredrawer and worker, a corn miller, and a gingham and check manufacturer.

Archaeologists uncovering the Chapelfield Dyeworks in February 2022 (© Salford Archaeology)

Excavating the Early Dyeworks

In January 2021 a sizeable portion of the site (1260m^2) was made available for archaeological excavation. The work uncovered significant structural remains of the Ardwick and Chapelfield Dyeworks, which were established initially as a single complex in the 1780s.

Elements of two buildings, revealed in the southern half of the excavation, were attributed to the 18th-century dyeworks of Edge & Beswick. The location and alignment of the walls correspond closely to the configuration of buildings shown on Laurent's map of 1793 and Green's map of 1787-94. Moreover, the hand-made brick and lime mortar used were consistent with the materials found in contemporary buildings across the river at Thomas Hoyle's Mayfield printworks. Parallels were also drawn in the scale and form of the buildings, which for this period were typically long and narrow.

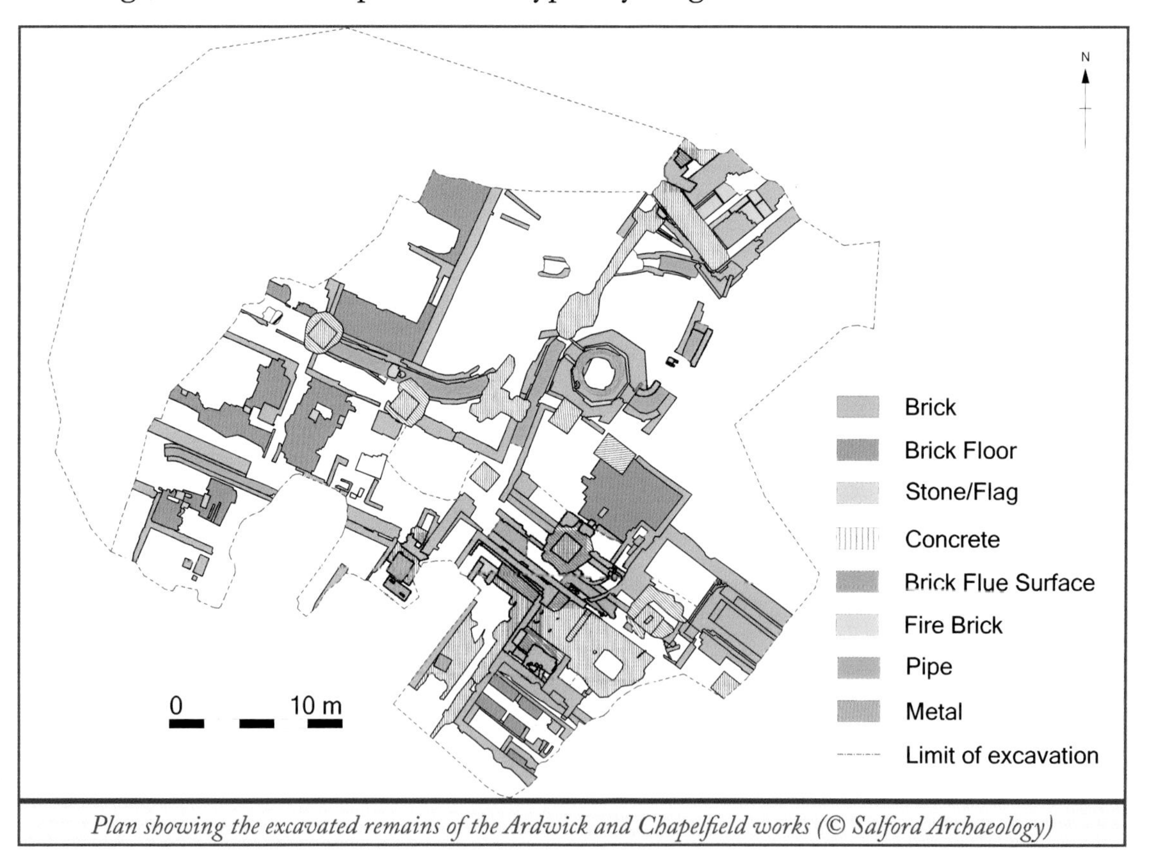

Plan showing the excavated remains of the Ardwick and Chapelfield works (© Salford Archaeology)

Block-printing was one of the earliest printing techniques and was most prevalent throughout Britain in the 18th and early 19th centuries. It constituted an important branch of the activity at Mayfield.

Block printer at work, note the suspended cloth above drying

This traditional method was practiced by skilled craftsmen using wooden printing blocks. The lower surface of the blocks was engraved in-relief with a design, which was wetted with liquid dye and pressed down firmly on surface of the cloth to transfer a colour copy of the design. The cloth was wound taught across the table and was attached to guide rollers at either end, passing fresh lengths to be printed and lifting the printed cloth to be suspended and dried from the ceiling.

This process was repeated until the desired quantity of cloth was covered. Small pin guides helped the printer to align the blocks, but care still had to be taken to ensure even coverage. The addition of each new element of colour to a design would require a different block. Sometimes as many as 100 blocks were used to layer up colours within a design, often requiring many hours work to complete a length of cloth.

The work was carried by an adult male printer, who would work at a stone-topped printing table. In 1846, it was recorded that amongst the 128 firms operating in Lancashire, there were around 7187 block printers' tables in use. Mayfield was recorded as having upwards of 150 tables in 1842, which were housed in the upper storeys of two buildings.

Block printer and tierer at work

The printer was normally assisted by a boy or girl, known as a tierer, who was responsible for topping up the tub of liquid dye and moving it along the printer's table. In the heyday of block-printing around 40% of the workforce at Mayfield was made up of children. A Parliamentary Commission set up in 1842 to examine the working conditions for children within printworks found the average workday lasted 12 hours. Whilst the working conditions of apprentices had been regulated under the 'Health and Morals of Apprentices Act' of 1804, wage-earning children were exempt and thus open to exploitation. Robert Hampsom a block printer at Hoyle's printworks considered 'the hours children [were] worked' to be too long. He often saw children falling asleep 'over the tub' and on occasion, work could continue for '24 hours at a time with the same teerer'.

Block-printing coexisted with mechanical printing for some time, only witnessing a national decline in the second half of the 19th century. By the time of the 1872 insurance assessment at Mayfield, all the block-printing rooms had fallen out of use and were described 'old' or 'disused'.

Major advancements in mechanical printing took place in Lancashire during the late 18th century. Thomas Bell was responsible for the introduction of press printing with copper plates in 1770 and the roller-printer using copper cylinders in 1783.

A visit to Manchester in 1818 found three types of cylinder printing machine installed at Thomas Hoyle & Sons. Only the newest machine was in operation; the other two were in reserve for when the main machine was undergoing maintenance. By the mid-19th century, a group of cylinder printers were running at Hoyle's printworks, and it was claimed they could print a mile of calico an hour. Printing had long been a male reserve. The successful trialling of female engravers at Mayfield was seen in the mid-19th century as quite progressive. They worked in the design department transferring the patterns to copper cylinders.

The drying room at Mayfield Printworks

A printing machine in operation from Barfoot's 'The Progress of Cotton' (© Yale University Art Gallery)

The Mayfield Printworks was established on the northern bank of the River Medlock in 1782 by Thomas Hoyle. The works were initially of 'small dimensions' but expanded gradually to become 'more like a small town than a single establishment'. To begin with the company was branded as dyers, although their name eventually became synonymous with calico printing, achieving brand-name status in the 19th century. Almost all facets of textile finishing were undertaken in-house, so that by the mid-19th century, the entire process from design to finished product, including dye production, bleaching, colouring, and printing was overseen by specialised departments within the works.

The interior of the dyeing shed as depicted during the Sultan of Zanzibar's visited to the Mayfield Printworks in 1875 (London Illustrated News)

View of the Mayfield printworks from London Road Station in 1894, by Henry Edward Tidmarsh (Image courtesy of Manchester Art Gallery)

Thomas Hoyle was born on 6th June 1739 in Rossendale, Lancashire, and established the Mayfield Printworks in 1782 on the banks of River Medlock on what was then the rural fringe of Manchester. The origins of the name 'Mayfield' are unclear, but it was perhaps chosen to reflect his wife's maiden name, Mary Fielden, whom Hoyle had married in 1764. Their son, Thomas, born in 1765, was inducted into the firm, which was listed as 'Thomas Hoyle & Sons, dyers, Mayfield' by 1797. The company was firstly established as a dyeworks, one of several located on this stretch of the river. By 1808, they traded as calico printers and dyers and from 1845 had specialised in calico printing. Thomas junior inherited the printworks after his father's death in 1821, and in turn passed the premises on to his three sons-in-law, William Neild, Joseph Compton and Alfred Binyon.

William Neild (1789–1864)
(© Salford Museum & Art Gallery)

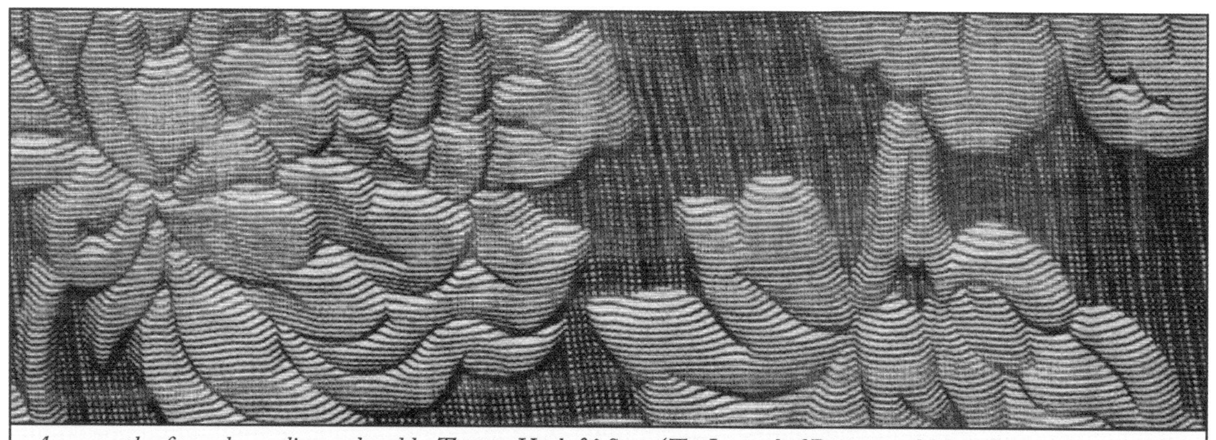

An example of purple muslin produced by Thomas Hoyle & Sons (The Journal of Design and Manufactures Vol. V 1851)
(© Salford Museum & Art Gallery)

William Neild married Thomas Hoyle's daughter, Mary Hoyle, in 1816, and had taken over the Mayfield Printworks by 1830. Outside the company, he took an active role in politics, serving as an alderman and as Manchester's mayor, 1841-2, introducing measures to improve the living standards in the town, and explicitly for his workers.

Hoyle Street, Manchester, 2022

Thomas Hoyle's printworks retained a foothold for over a century. As a consequence, long after the industry had disappeared, its legacy can still be found in factories, workers' housing, street names and public amenities that were left behind. Walls of some of the early 19th-century buildings flanking the river were still standing at the beginning of the site's redevelopment in 2019.

One of the surviving walls of the Mayfield Printworks fossilised within later standing buildings on the banks on the river. The walls were photographed in 2019 prior to the redevelopment of the site. The apex roof was a modern addition (© Photo by A Brogan)

Aerial image of the excavation of the Mayfield Printworks in 2020 (© Salford Archaeology)

Excavating Mayfield

In 2020, a selection of the buildings making up the former Mayfield Printworks was subject to archaeological excavation. The extent of the excavated area was determined by the proposed impact of the groundwork for the public park, whilst also taking in consideration the position of buildings shown on historic mapping.

The Colour Rooms

A long narrow building was exposed in the western half of the excavation. It was identified as an early part of the dyeworks and is visible on historic maps from the late 18th century.

One of the decorative cast-iron grates collapsed within the easternmost drain in the colour room

Substantial brick walls measuring up to 0.36m in width delineated the original extent of the building and its internal rooms. The north-western room was by the far the best preserved and retained a large area of brick flooring. The southern portion of the building had fared less well, suffering truncation as a result of modern disturbance. An insurance plan from the late 19th century reveals the building stood to three storeys and at ground level contained a 'colour room', 'colour shop' and 'colour mixing room', in which the ingredients for the dyes were prepared and mixed. Above were the block printing rooms.

A two-storey extension was tacked onto the north-eastern corner of the building and was built in several stages. The southern part of the extension was added before 1831, whilst the northern extent was completed between 1851 and 1872.

Floors and drains within the north-east colour room

The eastern half of the excavation

The eastern wall of the extension was initially built to a length of 9.69m and was eventually extended a further 2.87m by 1872. Unusual to its construction were four brick piers spaced roughly 2.60m (8 ½ ft) apart, perhaps fulfilling a structural role as the foundations for arched window lights, providing much-needed natural lighting.

A narrow strip of flooring survived across the middle of the room, hemmed in on all sides by drains. In the northern half of the extension, the drains were partly covered by three adjoining stone flags, which had six recessed sockets complete with upright iron fixings. It is thought this marked the position of an installation for dye preparation. Two cutaways within the flags acted as plugholes, emptying into the drains below. Elsewhere, the tops of the drains had been covered with perforated iron grates, which sat flush with the floor surface; these allowed for the run-off of liquid from preparation and mixing of pigments. Residues of vibrant purple and blue dye stained the floor surfaces within the building and had accumulated in the base of the drains, samples of which were tested for compositional analysis.

Elemental analysis of various residues from the Mayfield Printworks was carried out using a portable XRF (X-ray fluorescence Spectrometer). The dyestuffs collected in the eastern drain of the colour room had a vibrant blue hue and were found to contain notable quantities of lead, iron, titanium, potassium and sulphur. It is thought these elements may derive from the mordants used to fix the dye to the cotton, such as copperas (ferrous sulphate), iron liquor, titanium oxalate or alum (potassium aluminium sulphate).

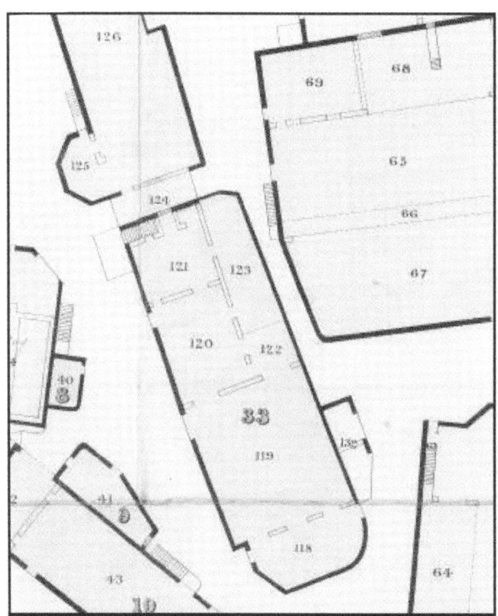

Extract from the 1872 insurance plan showing the ground-floor rooms associated with colour

Example of one of the drains stained with dye

Photo of Sample No. 1 taken from the drain in the colour room.

The Dye House

The central part of the excavation area was taken up by a large rectangular block of buildings with a date range spanning the 18th and 19th centuries. On the Ordnance Survey Town Plan from 1851, the main part of the building is annotated as the 'dye house', which despite its name would have encompassed a wide range of colouring and finishing processes.

Two of the stone vat bases exposed within the northern half of the dye house were inscribed with the initial's 'F' and 'A'. It is uncertain whether these letters were mason's marks or inscribed to indicate the contents of the vats.

By far the most compelling evidence for textile finishing were four large slabs of sandstone, interpreted as the bases of vats, in which fabric had been washed or dyed. Grooves around the edge of each of the stones would have supported the sides of the vat, presumably of wooden or stone construction, whilst circular plugholes set in the corner of the stones allowed for the contents of the vats to be drained away into the River Medlock.

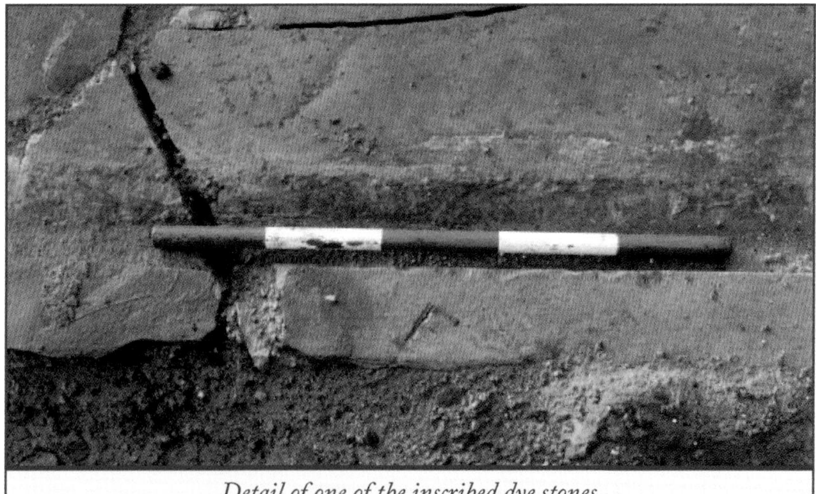

Detail of one of the inscribed dye stones

The surface of one of the stones was stained yellowish-green alluding to its potential use for dyeing. Lead piping connected to the vats seemingly conveyed hot water from nearby boilers.

A complicated network of interconnected installations, drains and channels were revealed in the southern part of the building. Whilst the exact function of some of the installations remains unclear, it seems likely they were connected with the soaping, washing or colouring of fabric, processes which are known to have taken place within building. Soaping and washing were both important operations in the final cleansing of dyed and printed fabrics.

At Mayfield there were at least two purpose-built washhouses, with additional rooms across the works dedicated to washing and roller washing. Soaping served to remove some of the colouring matter and to make the white areas of the fabric bright and clear from dye; this process was carried out using apparatus similar to a dye bath, in which the material was passed into a solution of soapy water. This was repeated multiple times, with sometimes up to six immersions. The process of soaping was mechanised in the 19th century and an entire room was dedicated for soaping machines within the Mayfield Works.

Example of Mather & Platt's dye jigger in which fabric was moved in and out of the heated dye liquor within the dye bath.

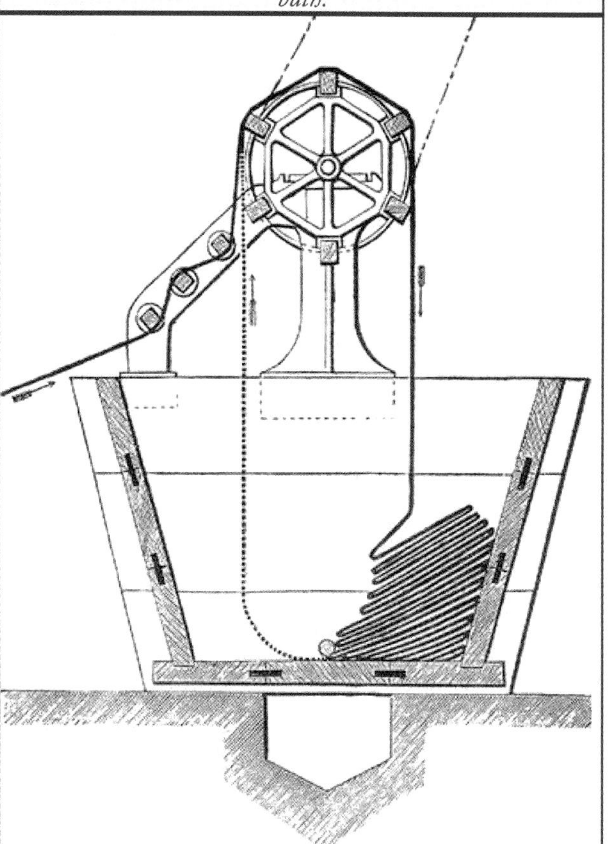

Diagram of a dye jigger showing the direction in which the fabric was passed in and out of the bath. Note the drainage channel below.

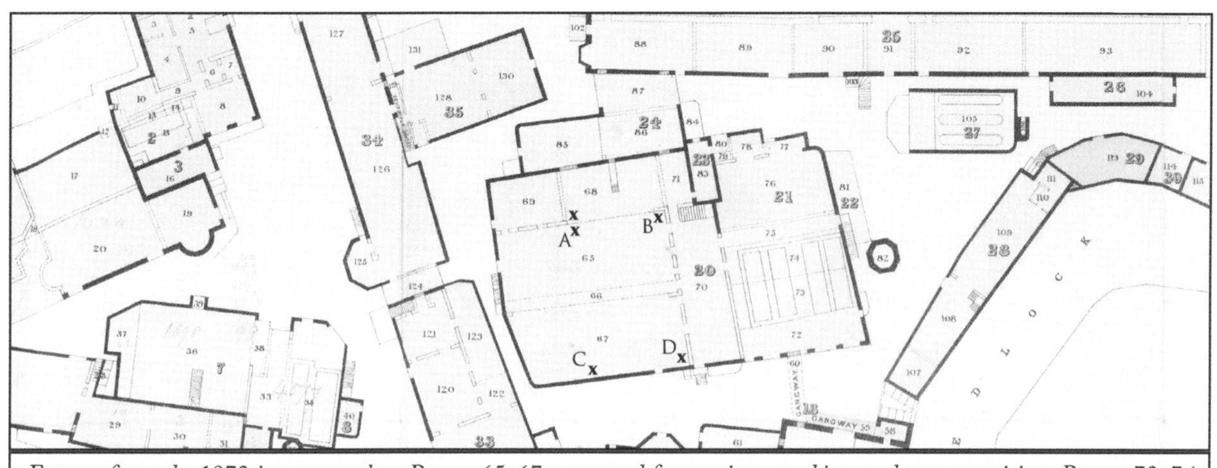

Extract from the 1872 insurance plan. Rooms 65-67 were used for soaping, washing and orange-raising. Rooms 72-74 formed the boiler house; the position of known steam engines are shown with an **X**

'Orange-raising' otherwise known as 'chroming' was a treatment used together with the processes of 'ageing' and 'steaming' to fix or develop the colour after printing. An instruction for orange-raising published in 1876 by Mr G. H Underwood of Manchester recalls the process was carried out in the 'fancy dye house' and that orange pieces of fabric were immersed in small becks with small winces (winches) fixed across them, otherwise known as 'wince dye becks' or 'dye jiggers'. The becks were filled with a solution of chrome salt, caustic or dry slaked lime and water, heated by steam and kept at a continual boil. After being raised, the fabric was wound round the wince to remove the chroming liquid before being drained and washed in water.

As more mechanised processes were adopted within the works, increasing numbers of steam engines were installed. Four small engine beds for compact engines were exposed in the dye house with an additional one found in adjoining room, latterly used as the 'print washing shed'.

Stone engine beds located in the dye house. From top left, clockwise: A, B, C, D

Left to Right: Example of a firebrick used in the construction of the boiler beds: 1.Lamb & Co 2. T-shaped boiler beds with the corner of the economising house and associated flue beyond. 3. Recording structures in the boiler house

Steam within this part of the works was raised by a bank of four coal-fired boilers, the remains of which were found in the eastern half of the excavation area. Though the boilers had long since been dismantled, they were survived by a series of brick and firebrick settings, a maintenance tunnel and associated flue system. Cast-iron doors from the boilers were recovered during their initial exposure.

The boiler beds had a typical T-shaped plan, set back from the front wall, to create a stoking or charging floor on the southern side of the boiler house. They were a form that could have supported either Lancashire or Galloway boilers, both of which were widely adopted the during second half of the 19th century; the former were patented by Fairbairn and Hetherinton in 1844, and the latter by William and John Galloway in 1851. Four Galloway and three Lancashire boilers were listed in the winding-down sale at the end of the 19th century.

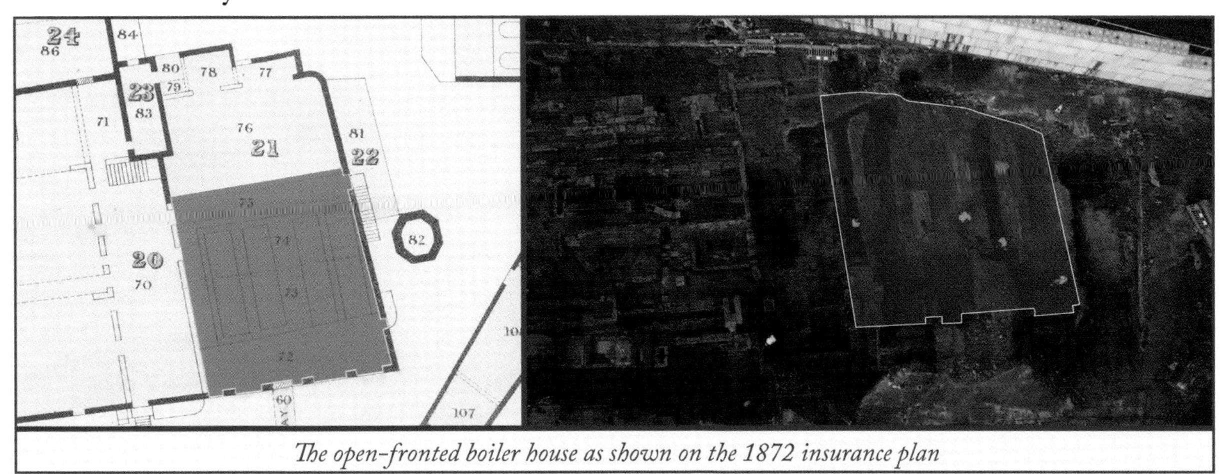

The open-fronted boiler house as shown on the 1872 insurance plan

Three successive floor surfaces revealed in the southern half of the boiler house serve to show how much the building was altered during its lifetime. The earliest floor was formed of stone flags and likely dates from when this boiler was added in the period 1831-49. Originally, the southern side of the building was open-fronted, allowing for the provision of coal. This arrangement was altered slightly in the period c.1849-72, when a sloping brick wall – effectively acting as a large-scale coal chute – was erected along the front of the building. After the sloping wall was built, the charging floor within the boiler house was also raised.

Sloping brick wall and raised floor surfaces within the boiler house

Broadly contemporary with these changes was another key development that improved the efficiency of the steam boilers. This came in the form of an economiser house, partially exposed in the north-east corner of the excavation. An economiser utilised the residual heat in the exhaust gases from the boiler furnace to pre-heat the water feed to the boiler and was typically made up of a series of metal pipes arranged within the flues between the chimney and boiler. The latest configuration of the economiser house at Mayfield utilised a 'Green's economiser with 192 pipes', which was recorded in the winding-down sale of 1897. Economisers were first developed by Green in Yorkshire in the 1840s and widely adopted in the second half of the 19th century.

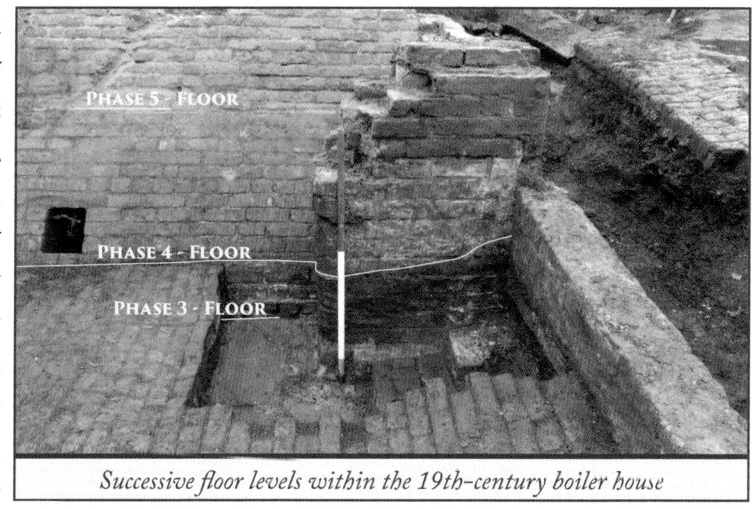

Successive floor levels within the 19th-century boiler house

Left: Eastern end of the boiler house showing part of the attached economiser room. Right: Green's patent economiser

The efficiency of the steam-raising plant was further improved with the installation of automatic feeders and a purpose-built chimney attached to the economiser house. The introduction of automatic feeders to the boilers was inferred from several adaptations in the southern half of the boiler house. The floor alongside the southern wall of the boiler house was raised up. The elevated surfaces presumably allowed the hoppers, positioned at the top of each boiler door, to be filled with ease from above. Around the same time, the façade of the boiler house was altered a second time with the addition of walls at a 49-degree angle to the existing frontage. Reconfiguration of access came in the form of a ramped floor.

Drone shot showing archaeologists excavating the boiler house. The position of the original boilers is shown in blue

EXPANSION OF INDUSTRY

Virtually no other buildings were erected nearby for nearly half a century after Thomas Hoyle and Thomas Beswick established their dyeworks on the banks of the river. The distinct lack of development appears to be in part due to the immense requirement of the dyeworks for space. Land on both sides of the river was taken up by large artificial bodies of water – reservoirs and filtration ponds – holding vast amounts of clean water required for dyeing and finishing. Higher ground around the dyehouses was used to dry cloth following the dyeing process. This was typically done outdoors in fields, known as tenter grounds, where finished cloth was hung from tenter hooks to dry. It was only after the drying process had been mechanised and brought inside that the tenter grounds disappeared, and the fields surrounding Mayfield could finally be developed. Hachured lines on Laurent's map indicate the former course of the River Medlock, which had migrated over the centuries; as such these represented less favourable land for building, and plots were slow to be taken up.

The next stage of the site's development commenced in the 1830s with the construction of Britannia Brewery and the Thomas Cunliffe's tannery. Both brewing and tanning depended heavily on a plentiful supply of fresh water, which was drawn from wells within the site. In the following decade, the Chapelfield Works was selected by David Moseley as a suitable location to base his waterproof clothing factory, which was soon expanded to produce all kinds of synthetic goods, from hoses and tubing, to telephones and tyres.

Extract from Laurent's map showing the tenter grounds associated with Hoyle's and Beswick's dyeworks

The process of turning raw animal hide into leather is an irreversible process. It is time-consuming, dirty and odorous. Unlike many other industries, tanning was slow to adopt mechanised processes, remaining strongly craft-based well into the 19th century. In Britain, the resistance and slow adoption of chrome tanning – a quicker automated technique – heavily influenced the decline of the industry, which was eclipsed by oversees production in the early 20th century.

A late 19th-century illustration showing the interior of a tannery (Source: Was willst du werden? Bilder aus dem Handwerkerleben. Berlin : Winckelmann [c. 1880].

Traditionally, raw animal skins were sold to the tanner with the horns attached, which were then removed and sold to other manufacturers. The next step was to stretch out raw hide over a convex beam, scraping away the outer layer of skin, together with any flesh attached to the inside with a long knife. The de-fleshed hides would then be steeped in a pit of alkaline lime-water known as tannic acid for a matter of days, loosening the hairs by the roots. Immersing the hides in this solution would allow the tanner to scour the hides. The scouring process was generally undertaken in conjunction with the initial cleaning; the final scraping operation removed the remaining hair whilst leaving the grain of the leather undamaged. At the Ardwick works this was undertaken in the 'tawing and scouring house' utilising both traditional stone slabs and machines such as 'Jackson's self-contained scouring machine'.

Once the hair was removed the raw hide was ready to be tanned, a chemical process to convert it into leather. The hides would be attached to a frame and immersed in a weak solution of water and vegetable matter, known as tanning liquor or ooze, which would be agitated constantly for a period of three months. Once the initial immersion was complete, the hides were transferred to pits containing a stronger solution of tanning liquor in which they were left for a longer period of time. The entire tanning process could take up to 18 months. Oak bark was commonly used as a tanning agent and was processed in bark mills, where it was finely ground up. One such 'bark breaking and grinding mill' was present at the Ardwick Tannery, indicating this preparatory process was carried out in-house.

Lime pits and rinsing tanks (Source: A Text-book of Tanning, by Henry R. Procter 1927)

Upon completion of the tanning process, the hides would be rinsed and smoothed before being hung up to dry, either in a loft or drying room. Part of the drying process involved beating or rolling the leather to compress it.

Tanning hides (Source: A Text book of Tanning, by Henry R. Procter 1927)

In the final stages of production, the leather was cut and shaped. This stage was traditionally carried out by hand but by the end of the 19th century, a wide array of machines were relied upon to cut, split and press the leather to the desired shape and thickness. Treatment of the products with dubbing and oil ensured they remained supple and did not dry out or crack.

Leather production was once a widespread industry across England and tanneries could be found in most towns. The history of the tanning in Manchester can be traced back to at least the 13th century. Around this time an individual called Hugh le Tanner owned property on Millgate, a locale which would eventually become a focus for tanneries in the following centuries. From historic records, it is clear tanning retained a foothold alongside other industries in the late medieval and post-medieval periods with the majority of tanneries being sited on the banks of the River Irk.

By the late 18th century, a handful of tanneries employed 11 tanners, all working within a short radius of the town's medieval quarter. The number of tanneries increased as the town grew in size. The rise of factories opened up new markets for leather goods, particularly through the production of leather belts necessary for driving steam-powered machinery. A contributing factor in the growth of this industry at this time was the reduction and eventual repeal of the tariff on leather goods between 1822 and 1830, which invigorated the trade, encouraging new people such as Thomas Cunliffe to enter into business.

Over time, many of the new tanneries were sited further from the centre of town. By the time of the 1851 Town Plan a total of 16 tanneries and skin yards were in operation, with concentrations around Red Bank and Deansgate; only two tanneries were present on the banks of the River Medlock at this time; the tannery at Ardwick was founded by Thomas Cunliffe & Co in around 1836.

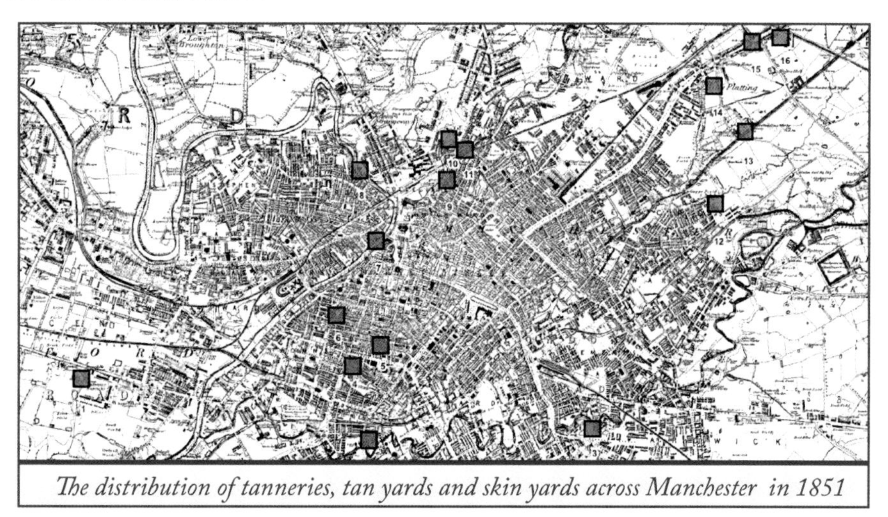

The distribution of tanneries, tan yards and skin yards across Manchester in 1851

Thomas Cunliffe's signature from 1815

Born in Yorkshire in 1794, Thomas Cunliffe was the son of a village carpenter, to whom he was likely apprenticed during his initial working life. In 1815, at the age of 21 and still a carpenter, Thomas married Mary Tattersall in Manchester. In the years that followed, he drifted in and out of several occupations, working firstly as a manufacturer, then as a waste and cotton dealer. At this time, Thomas lived with his family in Chorlton-upon-Medlock (then known as Chorlton Row).

From 1827, Thomas Cunliffe shifted from selling cotton to trading in hides and skins. The timing of this endeavour may have been influenced by the lowering of tariffs on leather goods in 1822 from three pence to one pence to the pound, which was followed in 1830 by the rescindment of the tax.

In c.1829, Thomas entered into a partnership with a smallware manufacturer, John Beckett, who was also a resident of Chorlton Row. Their names appear in Pigot's 1829 *Directory for Manchester and Salford*, trading as 'Beckett & Cunliffe' with premises at Back Alley and 4 Church Street. They dealt in animal hides and manufactured pickers.

of	Jane		[illegible]	Spinner	
Selina Ellen daughter of	Thomas & Mary	Cunliffe	Chorlton Row	Hide Dealer	[illegible]

The baptism record of Thomas' daughter in 1829 provides a clue of when he first entered into the leather trade

On Tuesday, the 4th May next, at twelve o'clock,
at the Brokers' office.
7000 Dry Salted KIPS,
ex A. B. Coutts, from Calcutta.—Apply to
JOHN and SAMUEL BECKWITH, Brokers.

On Tuesday, the 4th May next, at twelve o clock,
at the Brokers' office,
1100 Singapore BUFFALO HIDES.
Apply to JOHN and SAMUEL BECKWITH, Brokers.

Gore's Liverpool General Advertiser 22 April 1858

Not long after coming together, the partners sought out separate premises for a tannery, initially settling on a site on Berry Street, c.200m to the west of Mayfield. These premises were rented from 1829 to 1836.

From 1833, the name 'Beckett' ceases to appear in the Manchester rate books in connection with Thomas Cunliffe, replaced instead by Thomas Cunliffe & Co. The company was likely formed around this time, taking on two new partners John and Samuel Beckwith, who came from a mercantile family in Liverpool. Their father, Thomas Beckwith of the hide trading firm 'Thomas Beckwith & Co' was active in the early 19th century, dealing in products from as far afield as Argentina. The Beckwiths were brokers based out of Liverpool, effectively acting as middle-men for the import of skins, animal products and other agents incidental to the tanning industry. From the 1830s, they took full advantage of Liverpool's centre-stage in international commerce, tapping into trading networks across Europe, the Indian subcontinent and the Americas.

Example of a leather manufactory in Bermondsey, London

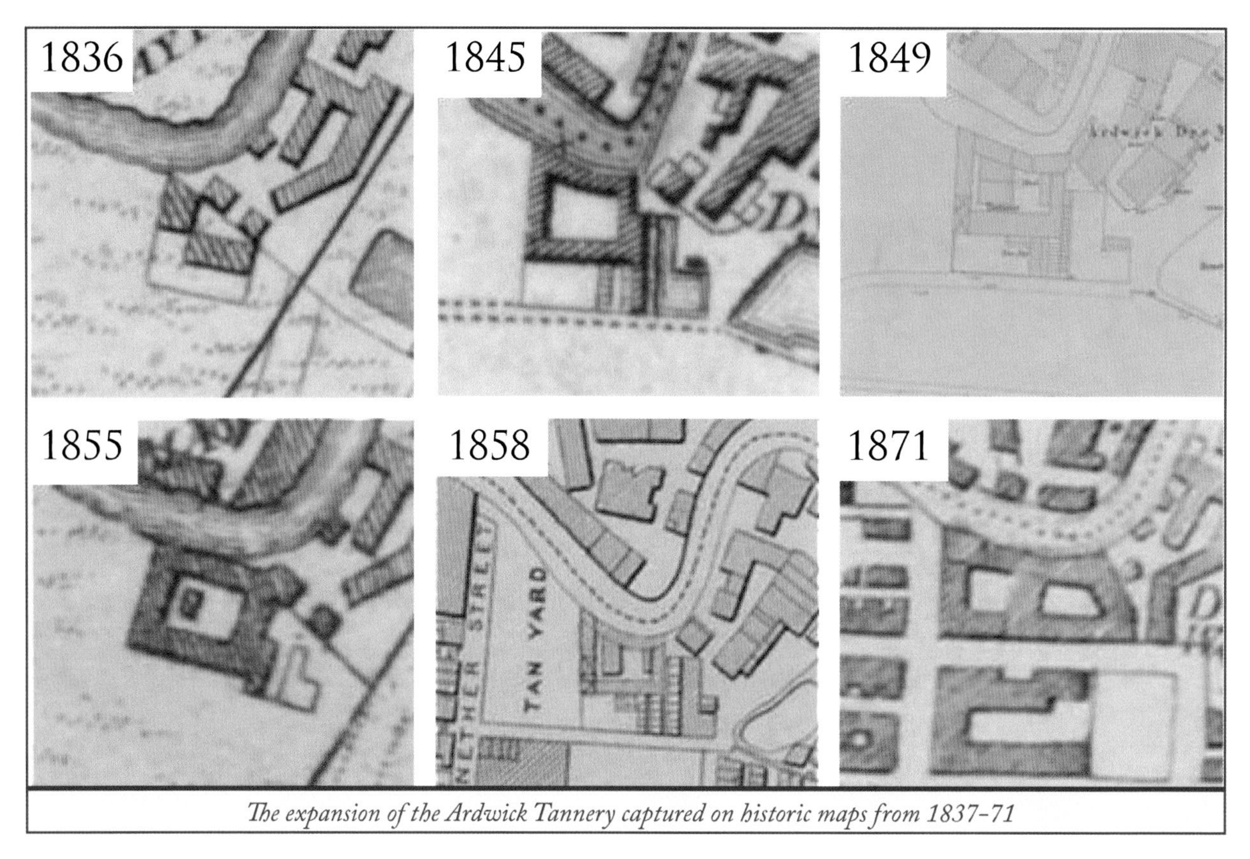

The expansion of the Ardwick Tannery captured on historic maps from 1837–71

On the back of several years of successful business, Thomas Cunliffe & Co purchased land on a southern bend of the River Medlock adjacent to the Ardwick Dyeworks. This was to become the home of the family business for over half a century. The first buildings constructed around this time appear on Pigot's plan from 1836. At that time, Cunliffe's premises at Ardwick were described in the rate books as a 'tan yard' with an annual gross rental of £17 10 shillings.

Extract from Pigot's A Plan of Manchester and Salford with Vicinities published in 1836

An initial spurt of growth occurred at the end of the 1830s, evident from both the available historic mapping and the valuations given in the rate books, which show a slight increase in the rental value compared to the neighbouring dyeworks.

Between 1838 and 1840, the tan yard rose in rental value from £60 to £80. Concurrent with the increased rates, the historic maps indicate the earlier structures had been pulled down with a number of new buildings being erected to the west of the original premises, forming an enclosed yard visible on the Ordnance Survey map of 1845. This courtyard arrangement was typical of early 19th-century tanneries, where many of the processes were carried out externally.

After roughly a decade, the partnership forged between Thomas Cunliffe and John and Samuel Beckwith came to an end, being dissolved in 1843 by mutual consent. This was a pivotal moment in the history of the company, allowing Thomas to formally induct his sons – John and James – into the business, thenceforth trading as Thomas Cunliffe & Sons. The Beckwiths continued in their capacity as brokers, and it seems likely the Cunliffe's continued to rely on the steady supply of goods afforded by their overseas contacts. Indeed, many of the advertisements for both companies indicate the trade and use of buffalo skins, which continued to be imported through the Liverpool docks.

In 1846, three years after gaining full control of the business, Thomas Cunliffe died aged 52. At the time he was residing at the family's second home in Warrington. Thomas Cunliffe & Sons passed to his two sons, John and James Cunliffe.

NOTICE is hereby given, that the Copartnership heretofore subsisting between us the undersigned, Thomas Cunliffe, John Beckwith, and Samuel Beckwith, at Manchester, and also at Ardwick, near Manchester, in the county of Lancaster, as Hide and Sizeing Dealers, under the firm of Thomas Cunliffe and Co. was dissolved, on the 31st day of December last past, by mutual consent. All debts owing to or by the said late firm will be received and paid by the said Thomas Cunliffe, who will henceforth carry on the business in his own name and on his own exclusive account.—Dated this 16th day of November 1843.

T. Cunliffe.
John Beckwith.
Saml. Beckwith.

Except from the London Gazette 1843

Listings in trade directories and advertisements in local newspapers across the country attest to the wide array of leather goods produced by the company around the mid-19th century. Much of their trade was dedicated to producing components for machines, serving to demonstrate how indispensable leather manufacturing had become to mechanised industries. Amongst the more mundane belts and straps, one product stands out, the 'picker' - a vital component of power looms. Thomas Cunliffe had seemingly been producing these items as early as the 1820s, but it was his eldest son John Tattersall Cunliffe who recognised the superiority of buffalo leather and made improvements on the design, filing a patent in 1847.

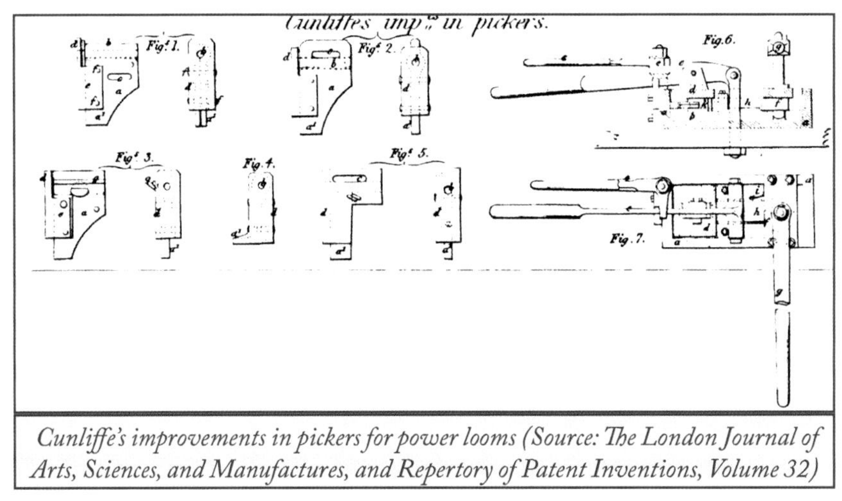

Cunliffe's improvements in pickers for power looms (Source: The London Journal of Arts, Sciences, and Manufactures, and Repertory of Patent Inventions, Volume 32)

As might be expected from the processing of animal hides, tanneries generated vast quantities of by-products. Lime-pit bottoms and spent bark generated from liming and tanning at the Ardwick site were marketed to farmers and gardeners as 'excellent manure'. The Cunliffe's also offered soft lime for the building trade, and 'first class hair' as an additive to wall plaster. Some of the waste products were processed further on-site before being sold, and from an early date the company was trading in size, made from a mixture of flour and tallow. Size was a valuable substance used in the cotton industry, smeared onto cotton yarn to increase its strength and tenacity before weaving. It was also found to alter the texture and weight of the finished cloth. In the long list of buildings in the winding-down sale of the tannery from 1892, the naming of the 'sizing house' confirms this product was produced at the site, once again illustrating how the Cunliffe's had aligned their trade to the mainstay of the town's economy, cotton.

The first detailed plan of the tannery was made around the middle of the 19th century. This shows the complex as it stood under the directorship of brothers John and James Cunliffe. It consisted of a series of adjoining rectangular buildings, surrounding an oblong courtyard on the southern bank of the river. The courtyard contained several additional buildings and a square 'tank' perhaps acting as a cistern for holding water. To the south was another enclosed yard with an entrance from Tipping Street, which contained a group of 30-40 interconnected 'tan pits'; these were arranged in rows on its eastern side

The configuration of buildings shown on the Ordnance Survey map of 1851 went more or less unaltered until an additional plot of land was acquired to the west of the works. The westward expansion began in the late 1850s, as evidenced by Simm's map of 1858, showing a large open tan yard, which ran up to Nether Street.

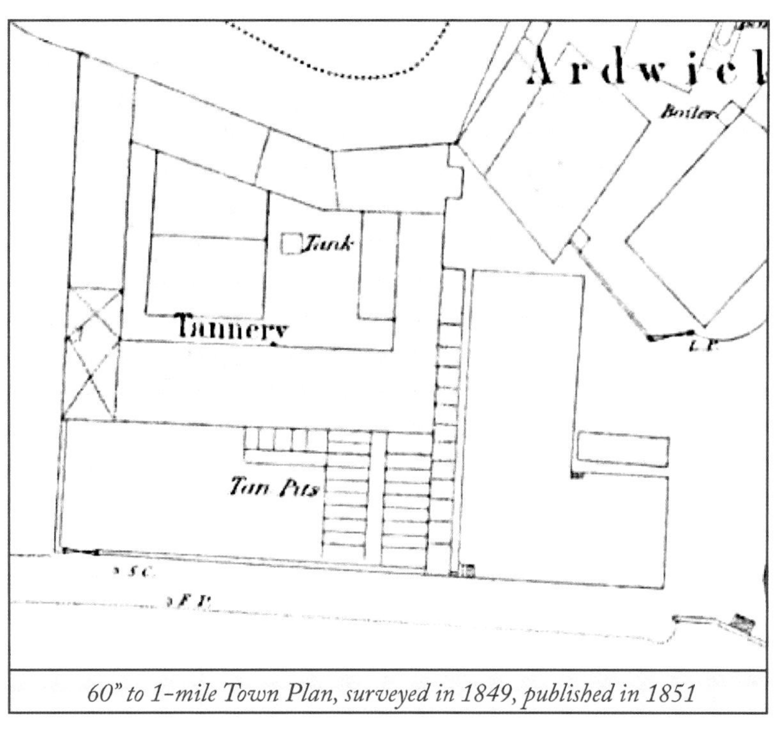

60" to 1-mile Town Plan, surveyed in 1849, published in 1851

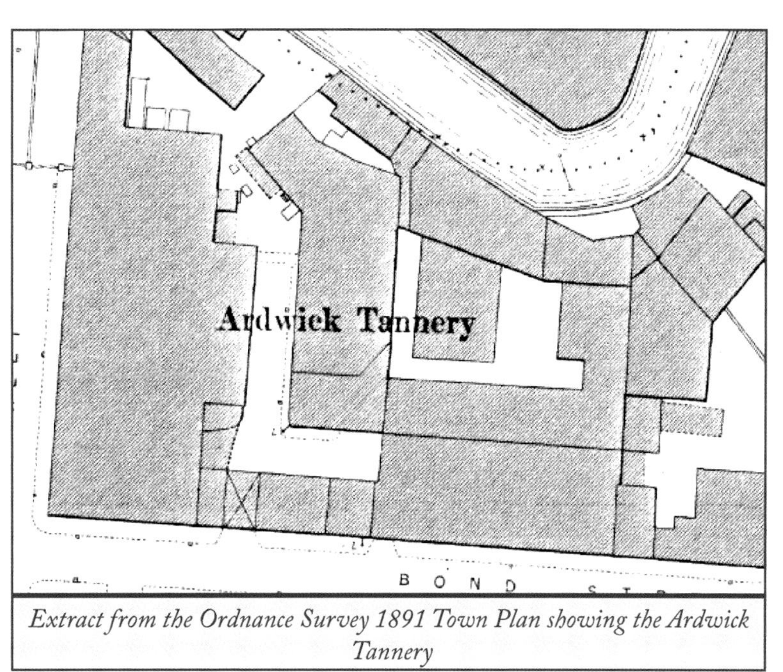

Extract from the Ordnance Survey 1891 Town Plan showing the Ardwick Tannery

NOTICE is hereby given, that the Partnership heretofore subsisting between us the undersigned, John Tattersall Cunliffe and James Henry Cunliffe, at Ardwick, in the city of Manchester, as Tanners, under the firm of Thomas Cunliffe and Sons, was dissolved on the 30th day of June last by mutual consent. All debts due to and owing by the said concern, will be received and paid by the said James Henry Cunliffe, by whom the said business will in future be carried on under the said firm of Thomas Cunliffe and Sons.—As witness our hands this 3rd day of August, 1864.

John T. Cunliffe.
James H. Cunliffe.

London Gazette 1864

In the space of three years, the tannery was beset by two near-catastrophic events. The first, occurring as a result of summer flooding in 1857, was more minor and aside from wetting 'a quantity of bark' any serious damage was avoided. Fortunately, the flood waters subsided before reaching the tan pits, potentially undoing monthslong work. In 1860, the tannery suffered a second disaster when a fire broke out at the premises. Reported on in the *Leeds Intelligencer*, 'much valuable property was placed in considerable danger' but owing to swift action, the cost of the damage was estimated to be £2000, a sum likely covered by insurance.

In 1864, after nearly two decades of partnership the brothers John and James dissolved the company, parting ways; James Cunliffe remained to oversee the running of the business at Mayfield. In 1867, John Tattersall Cunliffe went onto found the Holmesfield Tannery at Howley Quay in Warrington. This was later incorporated as the Union Tanneries Ltd and persisted as a business well into the 20th century.

During its final years of operation under James Cunliffe, the tannery at Ardwick witnessed a final period of expansion and modernisation. Between 1858 and 1871, the tan yard in the western half of the complex was enclosed by further buildings, bringing most of the once open-air industry under roof. It was also during this period that mechanised aids were adopted within the factory. The tannery continued to run until the early 1890s. In 1892 the site and contents of the buildings were offered for sale in auction.

In 2020, an area of the Ardwick Tannery accounting for roughly one eighth of the former site was subject to archaeological excavation. Although limited in its scope, the excavation demonstrated the survival of several of the tannery buildings. The majority of the structures encountered were erected in the period c. 1838-40 and were probably related to the arrangement of buildings shown on the 1851 Ordnance Survey Town Plan.

Although physical remains directly associated with leather manufacture were lacking, the excavation did successfully uncover the foundations of the boiler house and associated chimney. This provided a crucial insight into the steam-raising plant that once powered the tannery steam engines and, by extension, the machinery.

The excavated remains of the boiler house

The foundations of two boilers were revealed along the western limit of excavation, housed within a narrow north-south orientated range. The boilers had an elongated T-shaped plan and housed cylindrical boilers with a charging platform at one end. The 1892 auction notice described the boilers at the tannery as 'single-flue steam boiler, 16ft by 6ft diameter, with mounting; one double-flue [boiler] ditto, 20ft by 6ft 6in diameter, with [mounting] ditto, by Heaton'. Water for the boilers was probably drawn from wells. Differences in the specification of the boilers installed at the tannery imply the steam-raising plant was expanded gradually, perhaps initially with the installation of one single-flued boiler, presumably a Cornish-type followed later by a Lancashire or Galloway boiler. This process of development would be consistent with the growth of Thomas Cunliffe's enterprise over the course of half a century.

Stamped firebricks – bearing the mark of 'Farnley Iron Co Wortley' – were used in the fabric of two boilerbeds, providing further clues to the date of their construction. The Farnley Iron Co was a major producer of fireclay products in the second half of the 19th century. It was established in 1844 near Leeds (Yorkshire) and remained in production until it was absorbed by the Leeds Fireclay Co in 1889. Whilst it may be anticipated that existing stocks of brick bearing the stamp will have been in circulation after the company was absorbed, it seems likely these materials were incorporated into the structures at the tannery, c. 1845-90.

Exposing remains of the tannery boiler house

The chimney stack was of relatively small dimensions, measuring 1.45m across. In plan, the foundations were octagonal in shape, which by the mid-19th century was a common form for mills and factories. Although of modest size, the chimney is likely to have been large enough to create sufficient draught for the bank of two boilers situated nearby. Somewhat unusually, the chimney was not recorded on either the 1851 or 1891 OS maps, where generally such features were indicated or labelled, or perhaps implying it was not of considerable height, or perhaps being obscured from sight by nearby buildings.

The excavated remains of the boiler house chimney (1m scale)

Close-up showing the scorched bedrock base of the chimney

The primary source of power was a high-pressure horizontal engine, which most likely replaced an earlier engine that ran shafting and gearing within the works. Steam from the boilers also powered the donkey engine, a winch-type machine most likely used in the bark mill.

The application of steam power to the manufacturing industries saw the mechanisation of a number of tasks within the tannery. However, as a leading contemporary recalled in 1915, before the construction of leather machinery 'barely started 30 years ago…there were practically no efficient mechanical aids to lighten the exceedingly laborious operations incidental to leather manufacture'. The earliest advances were made with the introduction in 1818 of band knife machines that were used to stretch out irregularly shaped skins, and in 1856 with a machine that could split thick hides into layers. Most advancements came in the last quarter of the 19th century, as purpose-built machines were invented.

Several were listed in the winding-down sale of 1892 testifying to the mechanisation of the industry. These included: 'two of Jackson's self-contained scouring machines' used in the preparatory stage of scouring the hides; 'setting machines'; a 'rolling machine'; a 'striking machine' for pressure removing impurities from the leather; a 'leather belt callender' for smoothing or finishing products; 'belt splicing machines'; and a 'hydraulic press'.

Scouring machine by Haley & Co of Leeds, who held the patent for Jackson's Scouring Machine, which was listed in the closing down sale of the Ardwick Tannery (Grace's Guide to British Industrial History)

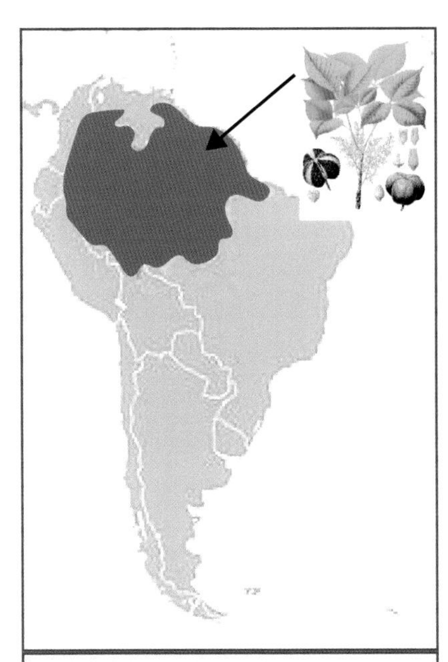

Geographic range of the rubber plant (Hevea brasiliensis)

Charles Macintosh (1766-1843)

The term India Rubber applies to the natural rubber derived from the milky resin of the rubber plant *Hevea brasiliensis*, native to the Amazonian region of South America. Natural rubber in its raw state had long been utilised by indigenous peoples of the Americas, but its full range of uses was not realised until the 19th century. The discovery of chemical solvents capable of altering its properties, and later vulcanisation, unlocked its full potential as a wonder material, permeating all facets of life, from factory to home.

Pivotal to its early development was Charles Macintosh, an inventor and chemist from Scotland. It was in Glasgow, whilst experimenting with naphtha – a volatile by-product of the coal-gas industry – he discovered its property to soften rubber. In 1823, Macintosh obtained a patent for applying this process to the production of double-sided rubberised cloth, sandwiching the malleable rubber between two sheets of cloth. He set up a small business in Glasgow for the manufacture of waterproof clothing.

It was only after moving to Manchester, however, that this invention was exploited en masse. Macintosh entered into partnership with the Birley Company – established mill owners – to produce rubberised cloth to his patent. In no time, H. H. Birley funded the construction of a mill on Cambridge Street in Chorlton-on-Medlock expressly for this process, which was up and running in 1824. Macintosh's naphtha solution continued to be made in Glasgow until 1832 and was dispatched to Manchester in barrels. Due to the uncertainty surrounding the scaling-up of this process, the mill was designed in a manner allowing it to be easily converted to cotton spinning should the venture prove unviable.

Initial production was not financially rewarding and was exasperated further by an economic slump in 1825. The process itself took time to refine and several methods were tested until the final version, using a system of rotating rollers and brushes, was perfected. A second individual, Thomas Hancock, ran into difficulty with the firm when his own invention came into conflict with the Macintosh patent. As a result, he was given use of the patent in agreement he acknowledged it, but was later taken into the Macintosh Company. After a fire at Hancock's London works, the firms were merged, and machinery was moved up from Stoke Newington to Chorlton-on-Medlock. The rubber works survived the economic depression of the 1830s and early 1840s.

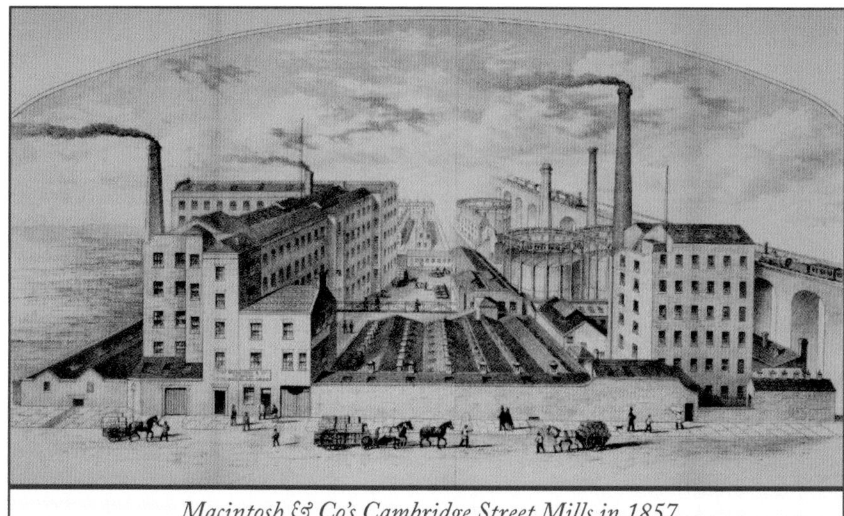

Macintosh & Co's Cambridge Street Mills in 1857

In 1843 Charles Macintosh died, leaving Hancock in charge. The following year, Hancock received a sample of vulcanised rubber – stable and resilient to heat – from an American chemist, Charles Goodyear. Hancock was able to quickly deduce the process behind it and succeeded in releasing an English patent before Goodyear. Having devised the process – a combination of steam and sulphur – a vulcanising boiler was added to the works in 1845, followed by a vulcan house in 1847. The pre-eminence of rubber to the business led to the cessation of cotton spinning between 1865-77, with a focus on rubberised cloth manufacture from 1885. By the 1890s, Macintosh began manufacturing tyres for motorised vehicles and were taken over by Dunlop in 1923.

An archaeological evaluation of part of Macintosh' works in 2001 revealed the footprint of the original mill basement and ancillary structures, including the power systems and rubber-processing plant.

David Moseley (1807-65) was from Cawthorne, a village on the periphery of Barnsley in Yorkshire. Like many, he was drawn to Manchester during the town's expansion. He worked primarily as joiner, residing on Rusholme Road in Chorlton-on-Medlock with his wife and sons, though it has been suggested he was employed for a time as a proofer at Charles Macintosh's factory.

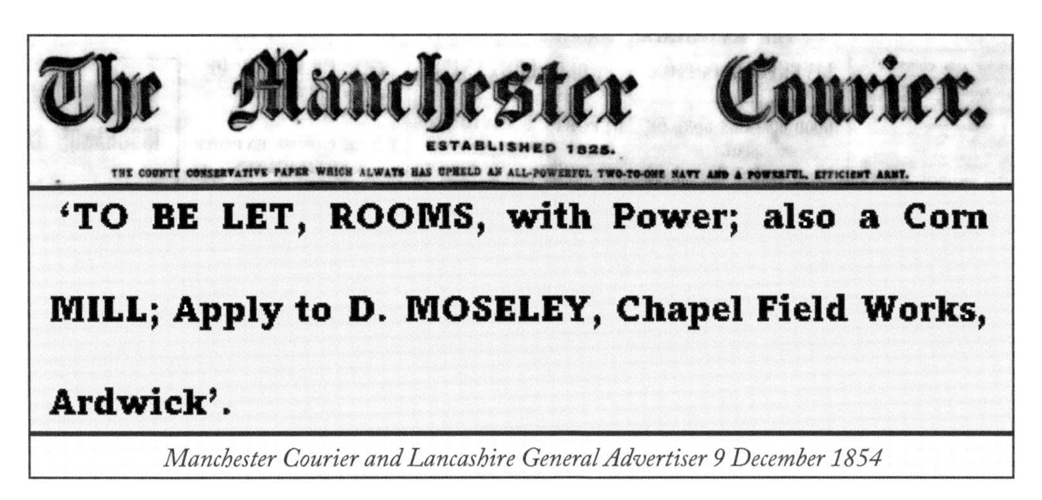
The Manchester Courier.

ESTABLISHED 1825.

'TO BE LET, ROOMS, with Power; also a Corn MILL; Apply to D. MOSELEY, Chapel Field Works, Ardwick'.

Manchester Courier and Lancashire General Advertiser 9 December 1854

His alleged time at Macintosh & Co may have given Moseley his first experience in the industry, moving him to establish his own factory producing waterproof garments. This factory started off as single room in Chorlton-on-Medlock and was operational from as early as c.1833. The Manchester directories show that he continued to rely on his trade as a joiner until 1847, whilst establishing himself a manufacturer. In 1845, he moved his garment business to the Chapelfield Works, which remained the heart of the Moseley rubber empire for nearly a century and a half.

Three years after the move, in 1848, David Moseley appears for the first time in the trade directories alongside Charles Macintosh & Co as a waterproof-clothing manufacturer. Surviving entries in the rate books from 1852-59, show he initially only leased premises in part of the Chapelfield Works at Ardwick, gradually taking on more factory space in the 1850s. Moseley bought out his partner and book-keeper John Chadwick in 1853, and by 1860 had gained ownership of Chapelfield Works. In the 1860s, he inducted his two sons, Joseph and Charles, as partners in the firm, trading under the name David Moseley & Sons.

SHEETS. WASHERS. VALVES.
CORD. TUBING. BALL-VALVES.
BUFFERS. DOOR-MATS.
DELIVERY AND SUCTION LINEN HOSE.
PATENT DURIFLEX and all other PACKINGS.

VULCANITE AND EBONITE. CELLUVERT FIBRE.
SHEET, RODS, OR TUBES FOR ELECTRICAL PURPOSES.

VULCANITE AND INDIA-RUBBER SHEET, TUBES, PUMPS, VALVES, BALLS, &c., for Chemical Purposes.

DAVID MOSELEY & SONS

CHAPEL-FIELD WORKS. ARDWICK. MANCHESTER.

WAREHOUSES :-

MANCHESTER :—2, 4 & 6 New Brown Street.

GLASGOW: 65 Virginia Street.
PARIS: 20 Rue de Marais.
LONDON: 51 and 52 Aldermanbury.
BRUSSELS: 14 Place Sainte Gudule.
BIRMINGHAM: 12 Easy Row.
SYDNEY, N.S.W.: 333 Kent Street.

It was during the second half of the 19th century that the extensive application for rubberised goods was fully realised; production within the city boomed and Manchester stood at the forefront of the British sector. Whellan's *Directory for Manchester and Salford* from 1853 lists Moseley as a producer of India Rubber and gutta percha – a similar plant derivative to rubber from Malaysia – used in making tubing, cord and as an electrical insulator. In 1858 and 1859, David Moseley took out two patents, the first for improvements for machinery in vulcanised rubber thread and second, for improvements in the manufacture of cards for carding cotton and other fibrous materials.

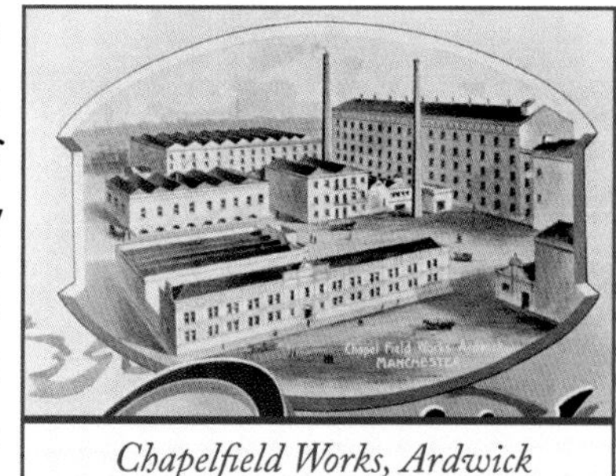

Chapelfield Works, Ardwick

Further details of the business can be gleaned from the third report on the Commission on the Employment of Children from 1865. The report reveals the average working day for women and children lasted 14 hours from 6am to 8pm, although no night work was carried out. Boys aged 13 to 18 years old were mainly employed in the laying and drying rooms whilst girls 12 – 18 years worked tying up elastic bands into bundles. The report shows that overcoats and elastic webbing were being produced on-site and that gutta percha was being used in large quantities. The writer of the report on Moseley's works commented on this 'branch of manufacture stating it is but yet in its infancy, and that ultimately it will open up a large field of employment'. After the death of David Moseley in 1865, his sons helped to develop the company, which branched out in several new directions.

Charles Moseley
(© Manchester Images Archive)

Under the sons, the Chapelfield Works expanded considerably, first by absorbing the Ardwick Dyeworks in 1876, the Ardwick Tannery in 1892 and Mayfield Printworks in 1897. This expansion is captured on a sequence of historic maps but is better reflected in the census returns. These show the scaling-up of the workforce across the town, which ballooned in the late 19th and early 20th century. By 1901, 30% of the national rubber industry's 18,516-strong workforce were concentrated in the Manchester area. In 1851, David Moseley employed just three workers; 63 years later, on the eve of war in 1914, David Moseley & Sons supported 2530 workers.

Charles Moseley took a keen interest in an emerging invention, developed in the late 1870s, the telephone. Realising its potential, he recruited engineers with expertise to deliver telephone services to customers in Manchester. David Moseley & Sons became one of the first British companies active on the scene, producing and installing lines and equipment for local businesses. As this technology was emerging, the company experimented with materials and techniques in an effort to improve their products and service, issuing no less than nine patents between 1879 and 1885 that were related to telephony. Although attempts by Charles in 1881 to open a telephone exchange on New Brown Street were quashed – the exchange was later taken on by the Lancashire Telephone Company – the Moseley's continued to trade as producers and installers of telephones until the 1890s.

Not long after, another invention, the tyre, sparked the interest of Charles Moseley, who together with his co-inventor Benjamin Blundstone began developing their own methods for production. They took out three patents for their 'India Rubber tyres' in Britain and America in the period 1884-9.

Above: Telephone transmitter.
Right: Gower-Bell wall telephone with transmitter made by David Moseley & Sons. Science Museum Group Collection Online. (© Science Museum Group)

In 1891, James Moseley and B. Blundstone filed an additional patent for an improved pneumatic tyre. These patents were taken at roughly the same time as John Boyd Dunlop invented his own pneumatic tyre in 1887, which became a favoured national brand. The Moseley's began producing and selling individual parts, such as tyre covers according to Dunlop's specifications, and as a result were brought to court for infringement in 1903. Whilst they were acquitted of the charges, the rivalry and tension highlights the economic importance of the tyre. The demand for tyres continued to grow with the increased popularity of the cycle and motorcar, the latter being an important factor in sustaining the growth and buoyancy of the rubber industry in the 20th century.

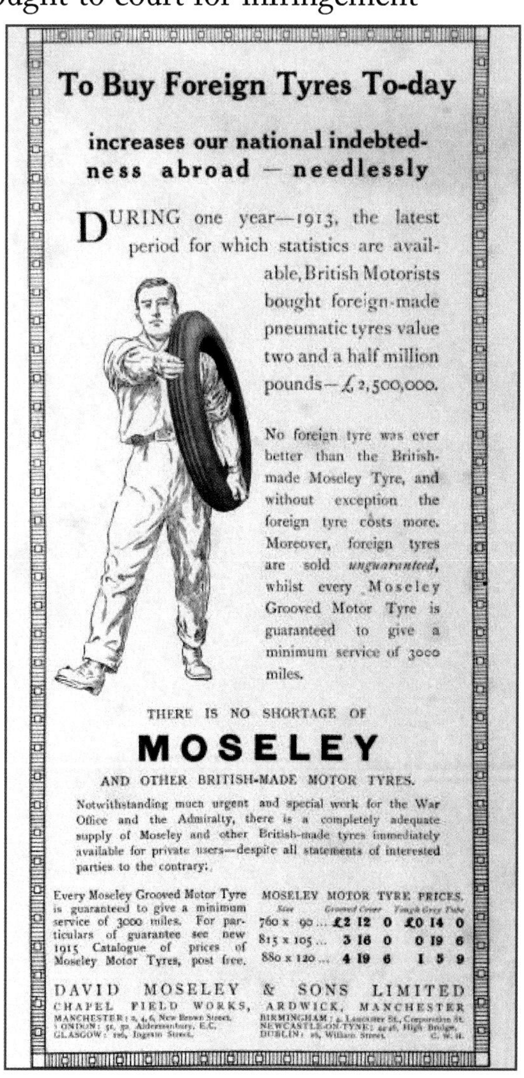

On the 24th of July 1902, David Moseley & Sons was incorporated as a limited company. The factory buildings sustained damage during the Second World War. The tyre plant building, which had been erected on the site of the Ardwick Tannery, purportedly received a direct hit from a landmine in 1940. In the post-war era, the company resumed normal production until 1961 when the waterproof garment branch of the industry was sold to J, Mandleburg and Co – a Jewish rainwear firm founded in 1856. The remainder of the company was bought out by the Avon Rubber Company three years later, who continued business on the site until 1981.

The Chapelfield Works retained many of the pre-existing buildings belonging to the Ardwick and Chapelfield dyeworks.

Many of the internal installations and remains attributable to the site's steam-raising plant remains dated to the mid- to late 19th century, after the original dyeworks had been taken over and expanded as David Moseley's India Rubber works.

The disturbed remains of a coal-fired boiler found within the Ardwick Dyeworks

The heavily denuded remains of a boiler setting were found in the eastern half of the excavation; the foundations were distinguishable by heat-affected surfaces constructed using hand-made brick and firebrick, some of which bore the stamp of 'Lamb & Co, Manchester'.

The last operational flue within the chimney leading south

The chimney erected in the late 19th century, likely after the works had been taken over by D. Moseley & Sons

The stone and brick foundations that once supported a horizontal steam engine

To the north-west of the boiler were the foundations of an octagonal chimney. The position of the flues feeding into the chimney suggest it was erected around the time of the works incorporation but was adapted and relined with one of the flues being blocked up.

An engine house and flywheel pit in the northern part of the excavation area probably supported a compact compound horizontal engine used for driving machinery within the India Rubber works. Many of the operational processes in rubber production were mechanised and this engine was probably one of several that were operational within the factory in the late 19th and early 20th centuries.

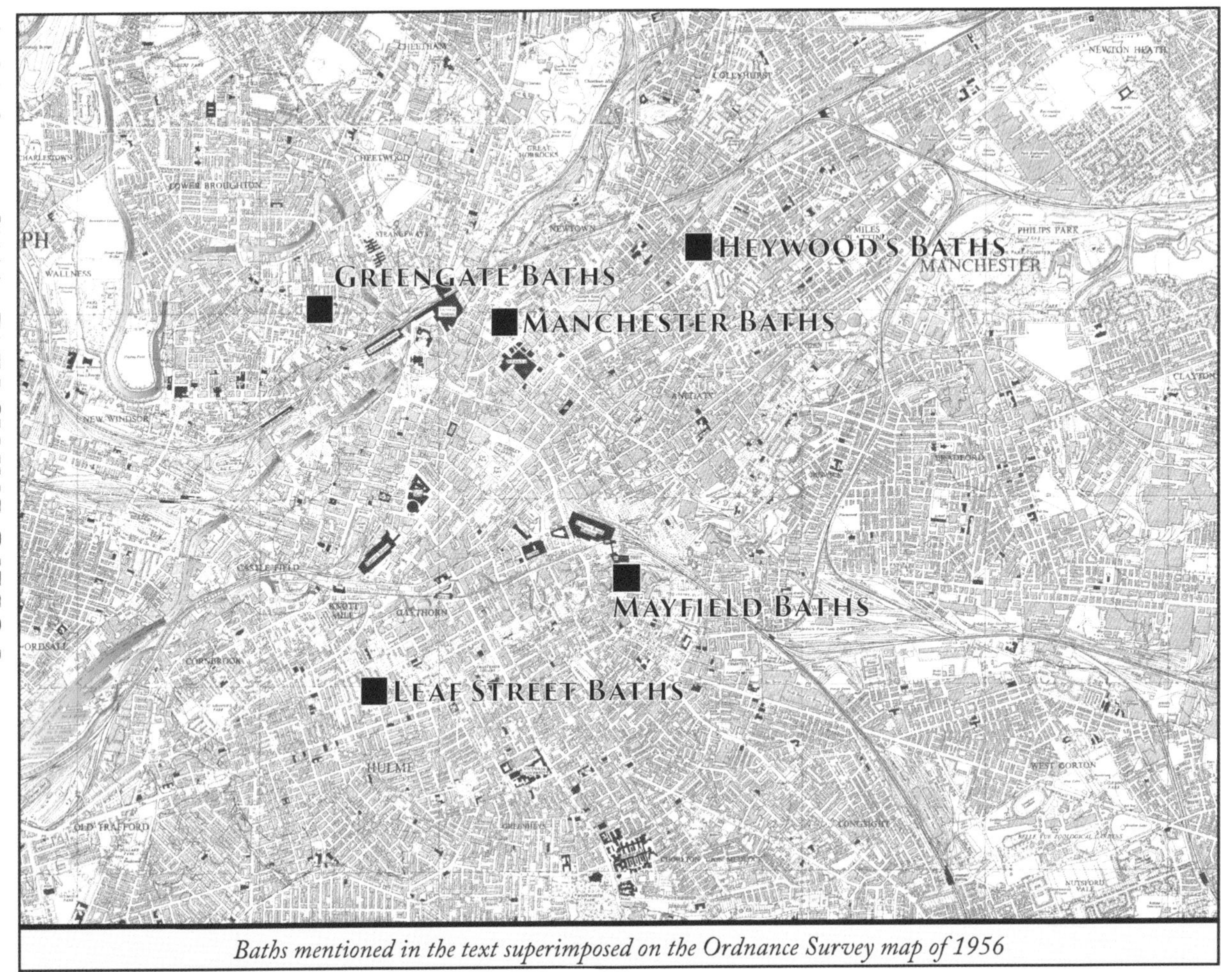

Baths mentioned in the text superimposed on the Ordnance Survey map of 1956

By the 1830s, there was widespread concern for the urban population in industrial towns such as Manchester. A large portion of the population were living in cramped, unsanitary conditions often without ready access to clean, running water. In 1847, only 25% of the town's 47,000 houses had piped water. Public baths and wash-houses thus represent some of the first civil engineering projects to be implemented to address the inadequate living standards. In Manchester, the earliest projects were pioneered by private enterprise. It took 30 years for the first premises to be adopted and managed by municipal authorities, and only after they had demonstrated their worth and economic viability.

One of the earliest baths attributable to private enterprise in Manchester adjoined the dyeworks of Frederick and Peter Longsdon on Tipping Street. *The Manchester Guardian* (August 22, 1838) reported that it was 'erected at considerable expense and intended for and used as public baths', although shortly after construction the owners fell bankrupt and were forced to sell their premises. The auction sales from 1838 and 1841 suggest the 'commanding and extensive' baths had served the community well, albeit for a short period. The baths were listed as vacant in the rate book enumerations for 1839-44 and were not assessed in the following years, suggesting they had been converted or demolished by the dyeworks' subsequent owners.

The Manchester Guardian.

'Also, TO BE SOLD or LET, all those commanding and extensive BATHS, adjoining the before named plot, which were and are likely to be much frequented.'

The Manchester Guardian August 22, 1838

The Manchester Courier.

ESTABLISHED 1825.

THE COUNTY CONSERVATIVE PAPER WHICH ALWAYS HAS UPHELD AN ALL-POWERFUL TWO-TO-ONE NAVY AND A POWERFUL, EFFICIENT ARMY.

'Plot of land adjoining the said premises [Messrs Longsdon and Company] with the buildings thereon, lately erected at considerable expense, and intended for and used as public baths, but which if required, might at small expense be converted into most convenient and complete workplaces for the above premises.'

Manchester Courier and Lancashire General Advertiser 25 September 1841

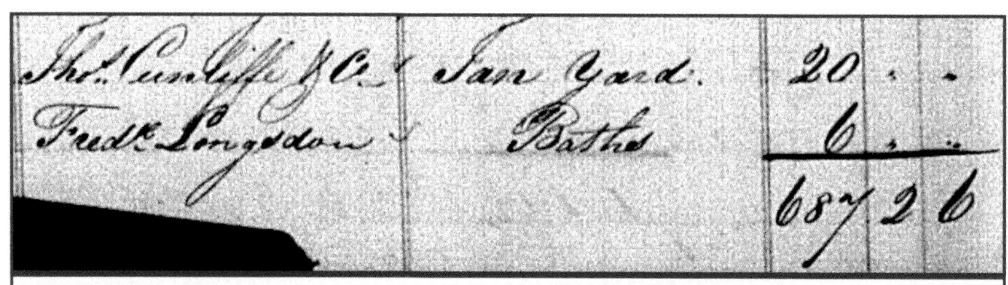

Thos Cunliffe & Co.	Tan Yard.	20 . .
Fredk Longsdon	Baths	6 . .
		687 2 6

Extract from the Poor Rate Assessments (1837) showing the baths on Tipping Street

In a similar vein to the Longsdon's short-lived public baths in Ardwick were those on Peru Street in Salford, funded by Thomas Bury, owner of the Adelphi Dyeworks. Although construction of the baths was started c.1835, there are suggestions the project was not progressed within his lifetime. Whilst the Adelphi Baths were eventually completed, they did not address any of the health concerns of the masses and essentially catered to the upper classes.

A major breakthrough was made in 1846 with the opening of the Manchester Public Baths and Wash-house within a converted three-storey, 12-roomed dwelling at Miller Street. Funds for the conversion had been raised from a ball held at the Free Trade Hall in the previous year, organised by the Public Baths and Wash-houses in Manchester Committee. The baths contained a department for washing and drying clothes and segregated bathing rooms for men and women. The facilities were well-received and, crucially, were financially viable. The owners petitioned for the Manchester Corporation to purchase and take over the management of the premises but were unsuccessful and were forced to continue self-funding the upkeep of the building until its closure in 1875.

Mayfield Baths photogrammetry using UAV shots. The image on this page is the men's second-class bath and the opposite pages has a representation of the men's first-class bath (© Salford Archaeology)

At the behest of another private benefactor, Sir Benjamin Heywood, a public baths was established on Sycamore Street in Miles Platting, opening in July 1850. It was designed cheaply by a joiner, Marmaduke Bunnell and was built primarily of wood, costing only £2000. It offered washing tubs for 45 persons, 23 wash baths (15 for men and eight for women, all of timber construction) and a modest plunge bath that was just 27 feet long by 18 feet wide (8.23m x 5.48m) but nevertheless represented Manchester's first public swimming pool intended for working men. Heywood's establishment proved very popular initially, attracting a total of 25,272 bathers in 1853 that covered its running expenses, although it was reported in 1858 that 'were it not for the interest taken by the superintendent, and tact in management, the place could hardly be kept open' due to the poor quality of the fittings and fixtures. The baths closed in 1869 as it had ceased to be self-supporting and, in contrast to the baths on Miller Street, 'commensurate advantage did not seem to accrue to the neighbourhood'.

Due to the slow uptake of the Manchester Corporation to address the issue of adequate bathing and washing facilities for the urban poor, a public meeting was held at the town hall to encourage potential shareholders to invest in a joint-stock company to fund the creation of public baths and laundries in Manchester and Salford. A total of 7,000 £5 shares were released for general purchase to secure the capital of £35,000 required to fund five new establishments within the following five years. The Manchester and Salford Baths and Laundries Company was incorporated by Royal Charter in June 1855. The appointed architect was Thomas Worthington. He went on to design three important public baths at Greengate (Salford) in 1856, Mayfield (Ardwick) in 1857 and Leaf Street (Hulme) in 1860.

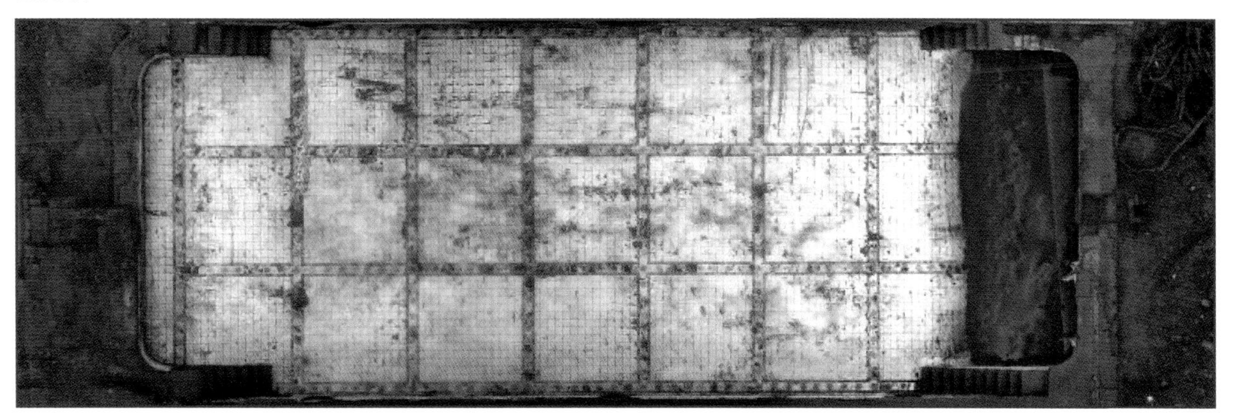

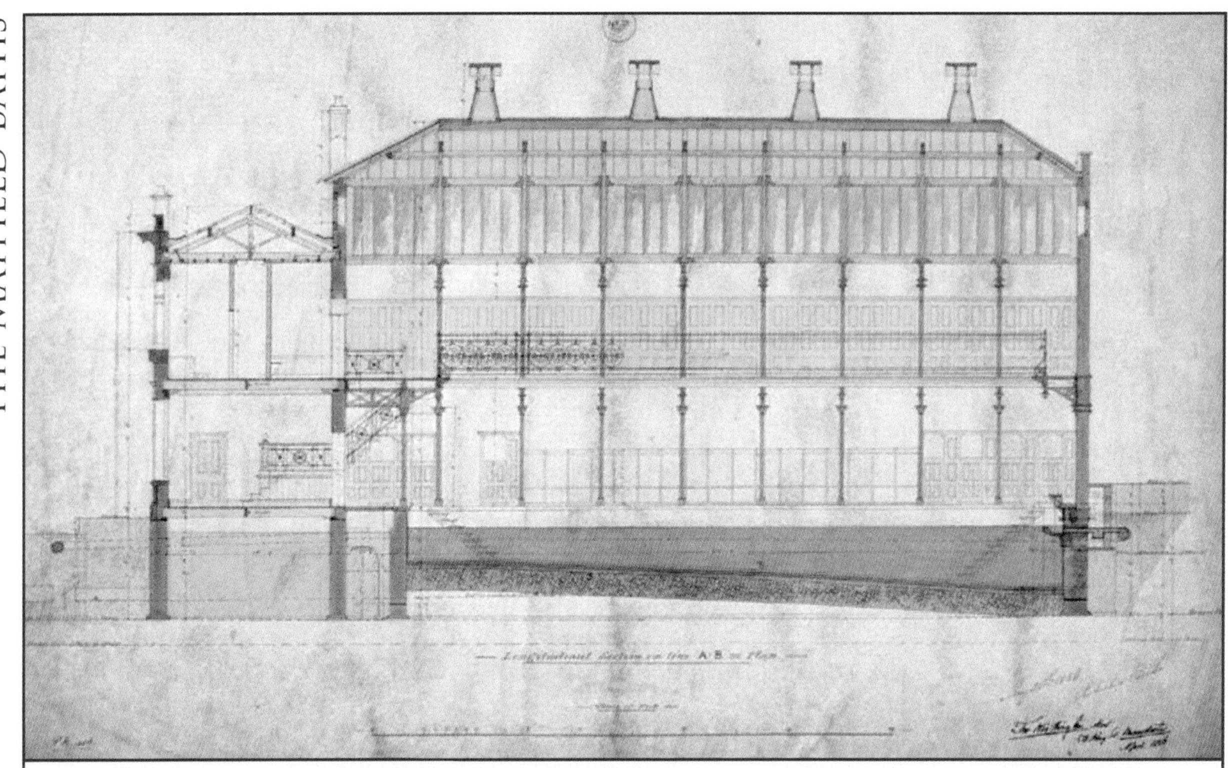

One of the surviving design plans of Mayfield baths drawn on canvas by Thomas Worthington in April 1856, showing the construction of the pool
(© The Thomas Worthington and Sons archive at Manchester Metropolitan University Special Collections Museum).

Opening in July 1857, Mayfield was the second public baths and wash-house opened by the Manchester and Salford Baths and Laundries Company. It occupied land in Ardwick obtained from William Neild, owner of the Mayfield Printworks, and a founding partner of the Manchester and Salford Baths and Laundries Company. The Mayfield baths proved to be a popular and profitable venture and the premises were expanded in 1860 to include the 'Penny Baths'. This addition had a pool designed for boys (4ft deep) and cost only one pence admittance. It was housed in a building on the opposite side of Baring Street. Due to complaints of boys begging in the street, the Penny Baths were converted to a subscription swimming baths in 1866, later becoming the ladies' pool in the early 1880s. In 1877, Mayfield baths came under the municipal ownership of the Manchester Corporation and were administered by the Baths and Wash Houses Committee, overseeing various improvements until its closure in 1940.

The Mayfield baths provided a much-needed amenity for those residing nearby. It became embedded in the local community, acting as a social a hub for those gathering to do laundry, perform ablutions and swim.

Washing and drying clothes ordinarily constituted a laborious and time-consuming chore, compounded by the lack of adequate space, ventilation and heating in most homes. The extensive washing facilities and hot air stoves – capable of drying clothes in 20 minutes – lessened the workload on wash day. The laundry also brought women together, adding a sense of conviviality to an otherwise lonesome task.

The swimming pools at Mayfield were also used for various competitions and activities that included galas, lessons, water polo, racing, diving, and even exhibitions. Enthusiasm for competitive swimming soon took hold and by 1870s, Manchester boasted two professional champion swimmers, rivalling London and the rest of Britain.

A key figure in the history of the baths and an early proponent of swimming was George Poulton, a famous ornamental and scientific swimmer. He was born in London, but eventually moved to Manchester, residing in Hulme. His spectacular athletic and aquatic feats, from underwater aerobics to drinking pints of milk underwater – gripped the attention of the nation. He used this renown to promote swimming and its health benefits to the masses and is regarded as instrumental in the development of professional swimming. Poulton first performed at Mayfield in 1858, a year after it had opened. He would go onto teach and lead events for over 40 years.

Left to right: Detail of boiler house chimney cross-section illustrating the position of the flues. Changing cubicles at Victoria Baths taken in 2022; note the ceramic numbers above the cubicles. The turnstile at Victoria Baths in 2022 giving an indication of the foyer arrangement at Mayfield (Stacey Johnson).

In 2020, the site of Mayfield baths was investigated by Salford Archaeology. The excavation was limited to the eastern and southern part of the baths, uncovering remains of the first- and second-class swimming pools and part of the associated boiler house. Two rectangular plunge pools were identified as the men's first- and second-class swimming baths. These were designed to hold up to 40,000 gallons of water, measuring 19.20m by 7.32m (21yd × 8yd). The foundations of the pools were well-engineered in order to remain water-tight and to compensate for underlying layers of soft alluvial silt. It was almost certainly issues with the ground that resulted in an unexpected outlay on materials during the initial construction of the foundations, costing an additional £970 (around £55,500 in today's money), half of which was paid by the vendor of the land, Andrew Neild. Layers of quarried limestone, concrete and brick – revealed within a sondage through the second-class pool – formed a suitably solid base for the pools, capable of evenly distributing the load of the baths above the alluvium. The pool walls were up to 0.85m (2 ¾ ft) thick, built from hand-made red brick bonded with hard, grey cementitious mortar.

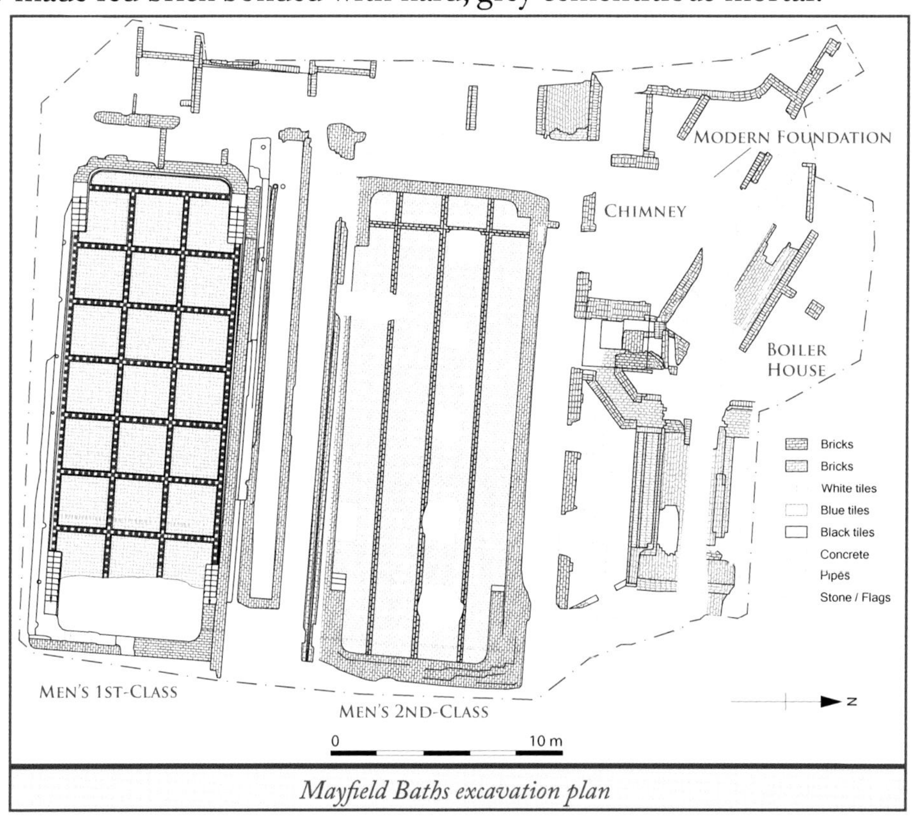

Mayfield Baths excavation plan

Sandstone flags originally lined the pool floors and were used for coping on top of the pool walls. The coping stones had a full-bullnosed edge and were laid with a slight overhang on the pool side. Circular holes in coping stones spaced at regular 2.35m (7 ¾ft) intervals along the pool side acted foundation pads for the cast-iron columns that had supported the galleried walkways and first-floor arrangements.

The men's first-class swimming bath in 1902 (© Manchester Archives and Local Studies)

All of the surviving tiles lining the pools were produced by Minton Hollins & Co of Stoke-on-Trent. These were not however original and were likely added after the baths had been acquired by the Manchester Corporation in 1877. Twenty years of use had rendered many of baths' original fittings in an 'unsatisfactory state' requiring £8,927. 4s. 5d. to be spent on 'improvements and alterations', including relaying the pools with concrete and resetting the sides with tiles.

The men's first-class swimming bath in 2020 (© Salford Archaeology)

During one phase of refurbishment, decorative motif tiles were added in the first-class pool. A slightly different style of tile had been used following subsequent alterations and were arranged in a grid-iron pattern on the base of the pool. Prior to this, it is assumed at least one of the plunge pools had been adorned with Italianate geometric designs visible in an engraving from 1858.

Extract from The Builder (1858) showing geometric tiles and open-tread steps

Black and white enamelled bricks by Gilmour & Co of Kilmarnock (Ayrshire) were arranged in lines on the base of the second-class pool, covering the original flagstone surface. It remains unclear whether the decision to reline the pools was driven solely by inherent structural problems or the desire to improve standards of hygiene, as ceramic surfaces were easier to clean than the original porous sandstone.

The tiles in 2020 (© Salford Archaeology)

Whilst almost identical in form, the first- and second-class pools were differentiated by their level of adornment. These three forms of blue patterned tile found around the waterline in the men's first-class pool were produced by Minton Hollins & Co (1845-1962) and were likely added c. 1877-9

Access into the water was afforded by solid steps with sandstone tread, situated in the corners of the pools. The surviving examples were not original and clearly abutted the face of the tiled walls. These steps replaced an earlier form shown on Worthington's original design plans. The replacement tiles used to in places to line the steps in the first-class pool matched those used on the floor, bearing a slightly different design and colour to the earlier two-tone examples.

Cast-iron spit troughs were arranged around the edges of the men's pools just above with the waterline. Five of the original seven spittoons survived *in-situ* in the men's first-class pool, taking the form of a half-bowl with a flat back affixed to the wall. With no associated drainage or apparent means of emptying, this early design may have resulted in the washing back of the troughs' contents, representing a serious concern for public health. Contemporary accounts recognised spit troughs to be unnecessary and 'a source of annoyance and disgust to anyone of cleanly habits or inclination'.

One of the cast-iron spit troughs surviving within the men's first-class pool

Ensuring a reasonable standard of water quality depended on the pools being emptied completely, cleaned, and refilled on a regular basis, typically once a week for the second-class pool and twice weekly for the first-class pool. Cast-iron grates were found covering the drain outlets at the lowest point of each pool. Corresponding sluice valves allowed the water to be emptied directly into an east / west conduit. This method of maintaining the water quality was expensive in terms of water, heating and labour costs, and was superseded during the Edwardian period by mechanical filtration and aeration systems. Experimentation with this technology was pioneered at Newton Heath Baths in Manchester in 1903-4, using equipment developed by Salford-based engineer John Royle. This plant pumped water from the deep end of the pool, aerated it via a large spray before filtering through sand and gravel, reheating and returning to the pool. In addition, the water was chlorinated on its return journey by forcing chlorine gas into the water at a point nearest the entry to the pool. This allowed the same water to be circulated, filtered and cleansed over a period of between four and eight hours, and dispensed with the need to empty the pool.

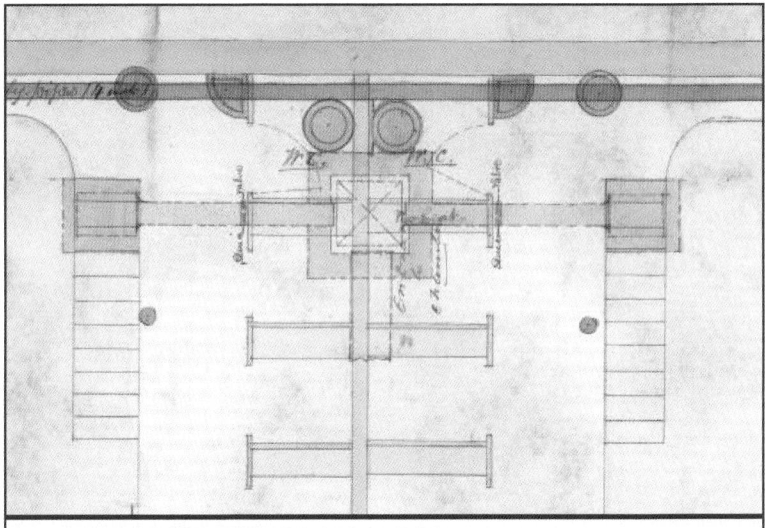

Extract from one of Thomas Worthington's plans of the Mayfield Baths showing the position of the drains in the first and second-class pools (© The Thomas Worthington and Sons archive at Manchester Metropolitan University Special Collections Museum).

The drainage outlet in the men's first-class pool

Collared cast-iron pipes (102mm internal diameter) set into the lower portions of the wall adjacent to the steps were presumably intended for pumping used water out, whilst small brass grates revealed in the walls at the foot of the shallow-end steps were likely installed for returning the purified water to the pools.

A Royle's calorifier installed at Mayfield Baths as part of the filtration system (© Manchester Archives and Local Studies)

Company accounts for 1913-14 record large sums of money – £401 1s 2d in 1913 and £827 5s in 1914 expended on filtration plant, suggesting it may have been installed at that date. A historic photograph of Mayfield baths features a Royle's water-feed heater, or calorifier, that will have formed part of the system, heating the aerated and filtered water prior to returning it to the pool. The photograph was reputedly taken in 1902, making this an early example, although it seems more likely that this date is incorrect. A small anteroom excavated to the south of the boiler room contained two rectangular stone beds fitted with threaded retraining bars that were set into the concrete floor, possibly representing the setting for the calorifier.

Stone block with threaded retaining bars used for supporting machinery within the anteroom

The hot water for the baths and wash-house was heated by steam raised by a bank of coal-fired boilers, located in the north-east corner of the baths. A complex array of pipes conveyed the steam, together with the hot and cold water to the laundry, slipper baths and plunge pools including the premises on the western side of Boardman Street, via a conduit built beneath the road.

The boiler house at Mayfield Baths showing two cylindrical coal-fired boilers (© Mancheste Archives and Local Studies)

Excavation demonstrated the survival of two boiler beds together with the remains of associated flues and chimney. The fabric of the boiler house implied that it had been heavily modified from its original construction, though the southern wall was unaltered. Parts of the chimney and early vaulted flues were constructed in hand-made brick, which had degraded considerably from use. In contrast, the boiler beds and unobstructed flues, operational during the final years of the baths, were constructed in a harder, more durable machine-made firebrick with concrete foundations, materials feasibly utilised during the renovation and improvement of the boilers in the 1923 and 1931-2, as recorded in the company accounts.

The entrance, waiting rooms and laundry were not fully explored during the excavation, although fragments of a cast-iron and aluminium turnstile lying amongst the demolition debris in the second-class pool gave some indication of the foyer arrangement.

Another interesting find recovered from the debris filling the anteroom of the boiler house were two enamel number plates that may have once adorned the doors to the private slipper baths or dressing rooms.

Left to right: The boiler house at Mayfield Baths revealed in 2020. Brick conduit connected to the boiler house chimney. The foundations of the chimney serving the boiler house, revealed in 2020 (© Salford Archaeology)

Mayfield Station opened its doors without a formal ceremony on the 8 August 1910. It was built by the London & North Western Railway company alongside the existing station at London Road (renamed Manchester Piccadilly in 1960) in efforts to improve their services.

Mayfield Depot, 2019

London Road Station had been operational since 1842, replacing a temporary terminus on Travis Street built two years earlier. Ever since it was established it had struggled to cope with the increasing stream of passengers and goods, and as a consequence witnessed multiple phases of expansion. By the turn of the 20th century, issues regarding its capacity were beginning to re-emerge; in 1901, around 20,000 passengers arrived onto the platforms on a daily basis, nearly three-quarters being commuters with season tickets. By 1911, the passenger numbers had risen to 36,341. Passengers were only part of issue. It was key destination for goods arriving in the city.

Mayfield Station was presented as part of the solution to this problem, easing both congestion on the lines and on the platforms by diverting local trains and creating more space for goods. A site for the new station was selected to the south of London Road but before the improvement works could begin, a 'vast amount of old and in many cases undesirable property' had to be cleared. In 1905, it was announced that buildings formerly used as Hoyle's printworks were in the course of demolition, yielding much of the space needed. Rows of terraced houses to the north of the printworks were also pulled down in preparation, displacing residents, who were housed in outlying suburbs.

Five platforms – designed for the longest trains of the day – were provided at Mayfield Station, three for goods and two for passengers. Below the platforms were offices and extensive warehouse facilities. By September 1910, there were 37 departures from the Mayfield Station on weekdays, and 34 on Saturdays.

With the outbreak of war in 1914, the station came into its own, serving as destination for wounded soldiers and civilians, and prisoners of war arriving from the front line in Europe. The first casualties to pass through Mayfield Station arrived in autumn 1914, coming mainly from Red Cross hospitals in Belgium. It continued to be used throughout the First World War receiving the injured for their onward journeys to hospitals.

Mayfield Station platforms in 2019, also showing hydraulic buffers

The station was hit by a parachute bomb on the night of the 22nd of December 1940, damaging the stables and destroying a signal box. After a brief disruption to service, the station and lines were back in action, and were again were used for the movement of troops and munitions. Normal service was resumed in the post-war years and Mayfield continued to provide a destination for passengers and goods.

During the modernisation and electrification of London Road Station, trains were diverted to Mayfield, then still receiving steam trains. In January 1958, British Rail announced that Mayfield Station would be closed to passengers and instead be used as a parcel depot. Mayfield closed its doors to passengers on the 27th August 1960, ahead of the reopening of the expanded and newly renovated London Road Station, renamed Manchester Piccadilly on the 12th September 1960.

Fuel pump inside Mayfield Depot

Mayfield continued to be used by the postal service as a parcel depot for a further 26 years, when it finally fell silent in 1986. Time and neglect saw some of station buildings fall into disrepair. Without the protection afforded by listed buildings status, demolition of the station had long been debated and by the new millennium, new plans were afoot to transform the site.

LATER DEVELOPMENT

Pockets of land within the site had held onto a small community of workers, residing in rows of terraced houses. The streets to the south of Mayfield baths and north of Britannia Brewery were designated as slum properties on a plan of Manchester's housing conditions produced in 1904. Another group of houses within the eastern part of the site, bounded by Tipping Street, Chapelfield Lane, Broad Street and New York Street, had formerly complied with byelaws but were nonetheless old and fast becoming dilapidated.

Although the India Rubber works continued to provide employment for those determined to stay, slum clearance was imminent. Some of the houses forming Indigo Street in the north of the site had been cleared before 1922 but most of the slum clearance occurred from the mid-1930s. Almost all residential properties within the site were condemned and cleared subsequently. As part of the initial investigation of the site in 2020, part of the site occupied by workers' housing was targeted by an evaluation trench. This trench uncovered remains of one the 19th-century dwellings that had fronted Hoyle Street.

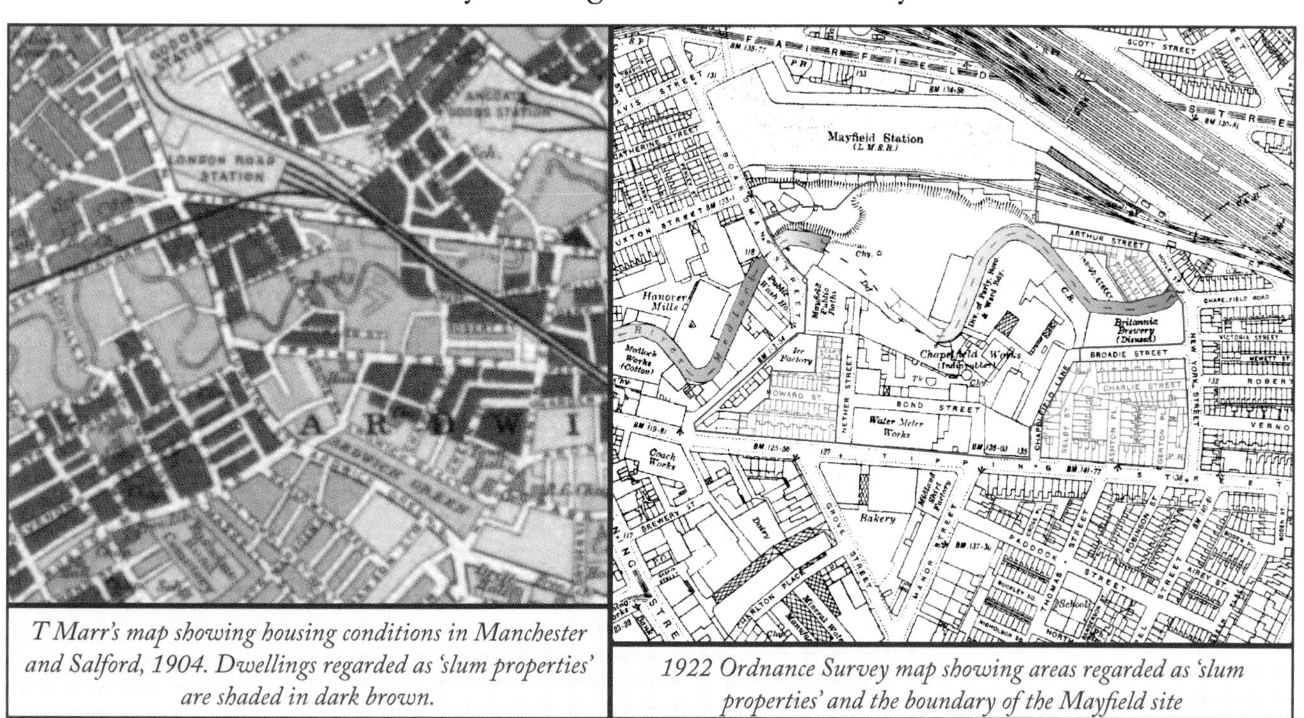

T Marr's map showing housing conditions in Manchester and Salford, 1904. Dwellings regarded as 'slum properties' are shaded in dark brown.

1922 Ordnance Survey map showing areas regarded as 'slum properties' and the boundary of the Mayfield site

A series of aerial bombings during the Second World War devastated the remaining commercial properties within the site, with hits on Mayfield Station, the India Rubber works and Mayfield baths. By the 1950s, a handful of the older buildings fronting Tipping Street were still standing; in the following decades these were torn down ahead of the creation of Manchester's inner ring road, the Mancunian Way, which opened in 1967. Additional low-level factory buildings associated with the rubber works were erected in their place. The closing of the rubber works in 1981 and Mayfield Station in 1986 saw these standing buildings fall into varying states of decay as the site lay dormant.

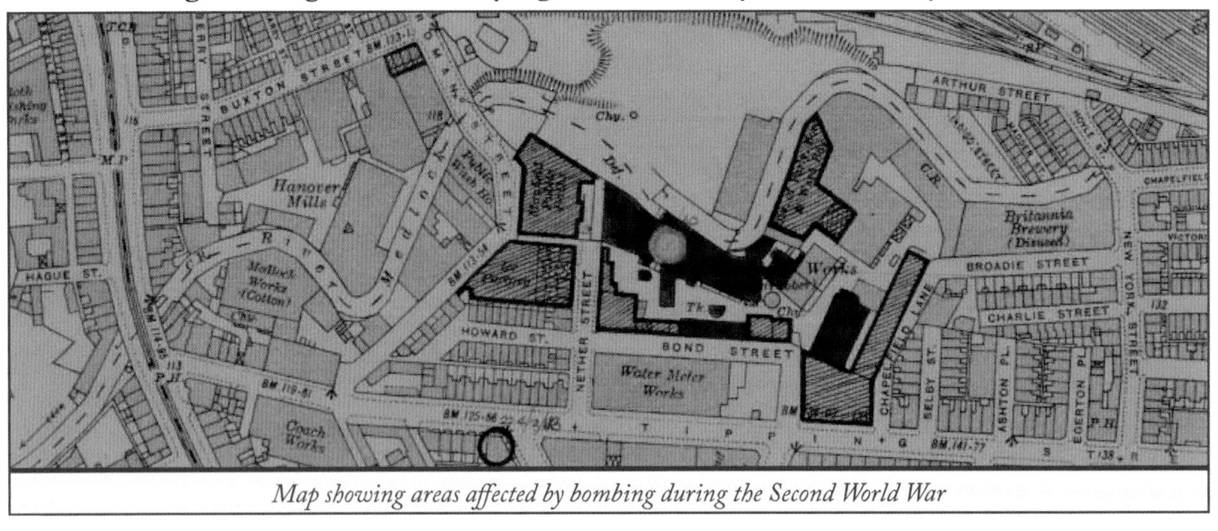

Map showing areas affected by bombing during the Second World War

Come the new millennia, numerous schemes were devised to repurpose the factories and former railway station. Consideration was given to the modernising the rail lines, and reintegrating the station with the city's rail network, whilst other plans entailed the demolition of the historic station altogether.

In 2013, the old station unexpectedly sprung to life as thousands re-entered its doors on a scale not seen for over half a century. This time, the dreary commuters were replaced with partygoers, revelling to the sounds and imagery of Massive Attack vs Adam Curtis. This event – part of the Manchester International Festival – showcased the versatility of the indoor space. Since hosting Manchester Pride Live in 2019, the station warehouses known as 'Depot Manchester' were given a new lease of life. Mayfield Depot now boasts a capacity of 10,000, putting on a wide range of music and arts events.

In February 2020, the proposals for the first phase of redevelopment were granted consent. Behind this plan were the Mayfield Partnership comprised of LCR, U + I, Manchester City Council, Transport for Greater Manchester. Work began in 2020 to regenerate the vacant land to the south of the station, building houses, office space and a 6.5-acre public park. The park was central to the scheme, serving the modern city dwellers, workers and visitors to the city. The tranquillity of the green space was achieved through cleaning up and re-naturalising a stretch of the river. Some of the newer river walls were removed and more natural-looking banks reinstated.

The archaeological works preceding the development, as recommended by GMAAS, were paramount to the ethos of the scheme, imbuing the park and buildings with a sense of place and providing a foundation from which to explore the rich history of the site. The investigations also fulfilled a planning requirement attached to the site, which ensured any archaeological remains at risk by the development were fully recorded.

Documenting the transformative process of the development have been a group of artists, photographers, architects and historians, whose work has elevated our understanding of site. Fundamental to this project has been Dan Dubowitz, whose aim has been to rediscover and retell Mayfield's forgotten past and present this accessibly to the public. Key events have been chosen and distilled into bite-sized stories, which will be transmitted to future visitors of the site.

Archaeology and groundwork in progress ahead of the construction of the park

Timeline

AD 1282	Ardwick first mentioned in the historic record
AD 1322	Lime kiln mentioned in Ancoats
C.1780	Edge & Beswick's Dyeworks established in Ardwick
1782	Thomas Hoyle establishes his dyeworks, later becoming Mayfield Printworks
1821	Thomas Hoyle dies, his son Thomas Hoyle inherits the printworks
1830	William Neild takes ownership of Mayfield Printworks
C.1836	Thomas Cunliffe sets up the Ardwick Tannery
1842	London Road Station opens
1845	David Moseley moves from Chorlton-on-Medlock to the Chapelfield Works
1857	Mayfield baths opens on Boardman Street and the Medlock burst its banks during summer floods on the 13th and 14th of August
1905	Hoyle's Mayfield Printworks demolished in preparation for a new railway station
1910	Mayfield Station opens
1960	London Road Station is renovated and renamed Manchester Piccadilly
1981	Avon Rubber ceases production at the Chapelfield Works in Ardwick
1986	Mayfield Station closes
2016	The Mayfield Partnership is formed
2020	Plans for redevelopment of Mayfield are endorsed by Manchester City Council
2020-21	Archaeological work is completed on-site
2022	Mayfield Park is opened to the public

GLOSSARY

- **ALUM** a mineral salt, commonly derived from iron-rich shale in Britain, used as a mordant for dyeing
- **CALICO** plain white cotton cloth
- **COPPERAS** a name given to iron or ferrous sulphate, typically derived from iron pyrites and used as a mordant to fix dyes
- **FUSTIAN** a thick, hard-wearing twilled cloth
- **FUSTIC** is a strong dark yellow dye made from heartwood of tree that grows in South America and Caribbean and was widely used from the 17th until the mid-19th century
- **HIDE** the skin of an animal, processed by tanners to produce leather
- **INDIA RUBBER** natural rubber derived from a latex-giving trees, mainly sourced from South America
- **INDIGO** a plant native to India and other Asian countries and forms a blue dye
- **LINEN** cloth woven from flax
- **MADDER** a red dye from the roots of the madder plant, imported mainly from the Middle East
- **MACINTOSH** raincoat named after Charles Macintosh, the Scottish inventor of the waterproof material used to make the garments
- **MORDANT** a substance used to fix dyes to fabric
- **PUBLIC BATHS** privately or municipally owned building, open to the public with facilities for bathing, often containing large pools for swimming
- **WASH HOUSE** building serving as a laundry, often associated with bathing facilities

FURTHER READING

- Fletcher K, and Miller I, 2022 *Douglas Green, Pendleton: The Archaeology of an Industrial Colony,* Greater Manchester's Past Revealed, 30, Manchester

- Hancock, T, 1857 *Personal Narrative of the Origin and Progress of the Caoutchouc or India-Rubber Manufacture in England,* Longman, Brown, Green, Longmans, & Roberts, London

- Miller, I, 2012 *An Industrial Art: The Archaeology of Calico Printing in the Irwell Valley,* Greater Manchester's Past Revealed, 6, Lancaster

- Miller, I, and Cook, O, 2021 *Coming Out in the Wash: Investigating Manchester's Public Baths and Wash-houses*, Industrial Archaeology Review, 43 (2), 114-34 https://doi.org/10.1080/03090728.2021.1967572

- Sykas, PA, 2022 *Pathways in the Nineteenth-Century British Textile Industry,* Routledge, London

- Wright, T, 2013 *Thomas Hoyle and the Mayfield Print Works*, Manchester

Most of the historical maps used in this booklet can be found at Manchester Archives and Local Studies in Manchester Central Library, and at Salford Local History Library in Salford Museum and Art Gallery.

Copies of the detailed technical reports from the excavations by Salford Archaeology have been deposited with the Greater Manchester Historic Environment Record.

Publications in the *Greater Manchester's Past Revealed* series are available from GMAAS within the University of Salford, and digital copies of all the volumes published between 2010 and 2021 can be downloaded at https://gmaas.salford.ac.uk/publications/